MACHINE STITCHERY

MACHINE STITCHERY

Gay Swift

B T BATSFORD LTD   LONDON AND SYDNEY

For G T

© Gay Swift 1974
First published 1974
ISBN 0 7134 2883 X

Designed by Charlotte Gerlings
Set in Monophoto Times New Roman (327)
9 on 11 point by
Servis Filmsetting Limited, Manchester
Printed in Great Britain by
William Clowes and Sons Limited
Beccles, Suffolk
for the publishers
B T Batsford Limited
4 Fitzhardinge Street, London W1H 0AH and
23 Cross Street, PO Box 586
Brookvale, NSW 2100, Australia

Contents

Acknowledgment

My thanks are due to the following for advice and help:
Abel Morrall Limited, Dorothy Benson, Jenny Gray, Barbara
Wright, Coats Sewing Group, David Williams, Stanley
Claughton, The Tolson Memorial Museum Huddersfield,
Bradford Central Library, The Science Museum London,
The Metropolitan Museum of Art New York, Judi Lewis,
Tajinder Saund, Celia Wilson, Claire Wilson, and Thelma
M. Nye.

Introduction

The word *embroidery* must be used progressively more loosely to include anything which applies one textile quality to another.

Machine embroidery is the process of decorating textile surfaces by means of machine stitching. At its most basic it may consist of parallel stitched lines at a seam, or at its most adventurous it may be used to apply an elaborate variety of raised surfaces to a background fabric. The embroiderer with automatic needle and electric motor is just as much in control as the graphic designer with air brush and compressor.

It is not an imitator of hand embroidery neither is it a competitor. As an additional technique of construction and surface enrichment it has brought a strong new influence into textile decoration.

Mass production machine embroidery was born in 1828 as a result of ideal conditions. The single head sewing machine had begun to develop, and M Josué Heilmann of Mulhouse, amongst others, saw the possibility of working many needles instead of one and therefore satisfying the increasing demand for opulent fabrics (although strangely, mass produced embroidery stimulated the demand for hand embroidery), as well as avoiding the rising cost of skilled labour. One of the basic principles, sewing with a needle with a central eye and a point at each end, had been invented in 1775 by Weisenthal. The machines were first used to produce coloured floral designs in silks on satin, but by the 1830s they had been sufficiently modified to imitate delicate white *Swiss* embroidery on fine cottons.

In the early 1830s Walter Hunt invented the first single head lock stitch machine which used a needle thread above the fabric and a shuttle below it, but this idea was not patented until Elias Howe's machine in 1846. But both inventions had strict practical limitations. In 1851 Isaac M. Singer designed a machine with most of the basic features familiar today.

It is not clear when free stitching began, but in a report on the French textiles shown at the Paris Exhibition in 1878 M Théodore Biais mentioned some pieces and commented on the likelihood of its eventual development. Some ambitious pictures worked before World War I reproduce landscape paintings in considerable detail. Two factors delayed the creative development of single head machine embroidery, however; machines were expected to reproduce hand embroidery and lace making techniques, which the domestic lock stitch could not accomplish as well as the multiples: and, without electricity, freedom of line was severely limited.

After thirty years of experiment Singer evolved the first portable electric machine in 1921, when the possibilities of free stitching became more available. The Singer Sewing Machine Company and Miss Dorothy Benson were largely responsible for promoting free stitchery in the twenties and thirties through instructive publications.

Machine embroidery has been compared to drawing, but there are several essential differences between the techniques of drawing and machine stitching. The draughtsman uses tools held in the hand and moves them over a static surface, while the machine embroiderer moves the surface to be decorated appropriately to the fixed position of the needle. Drawing produces a line or texture of infinitely variable pressure, speed, direction and length, while a machine embroidered line is much less flexible. Drawn marks can vary in length but a machined line should be considered as continuous. For these reasons, although the machine is simply another medium, its limitations must be realised before its potential is exploited. In imitation of other media it is at its worst, but used with care and sensitivity it is a fluent form of expression.

Because it demands a sophisticated level of coordination between both hands, both feet and both eyes it is not suitable for young children. For older children, apart from its obvious possibilities as an expressive medium, it is a good way of learning to use a machine as a physical extension of oneself, rather than a mysterious object to be battled with. For this reason those people who regard machinery with a sort of inborn mistrust are unlikely to be at ease, while those who work with machines or just simply drive competently have an advantage.

Saint's sewing machine 1790. *Crown copyright, Science Museum, London*

The Moldacot travelling chain stitch machine. *Courtesy Tolson Memorial Museum, Huddersfield*

A sewing machine is capable of many decorative techniques without any adjustment, and these can be achieved on a treadle machine or even one which is hand driven: but for what is clumsily referred to as *free hand machine embroidery* an electrically driven machine is essential. Also the feed dog must be put out of action in some way, and this can be done by lowering it either automatically or manually, but on some older, cheaper or lightweight machines there is no means of doing this. In these cases the manufacturer may include a feed cover plate in the accessories or make one as an optional extra, or the throat plate can be raised to clear the feed (described on page 28). Treadles converted by the addition of an electric motor or modern machines set into old treadle stands are the best for machine embroidery, because they can be controlled with one foot used to speed up the machine and the other placed behind it to slow the machine down. This is much more sensitive than the tiny surface area for foot control on modern portables. A requirement of any good sewing machine is that it should have a smooth, unhurried start and be controllable at very slow speeds. Old machines with long shuttles are not suitable for free stitching.

There are photographs of several old machines, for historical interest and as an indication that embroidery is possible on any machine. Modern machines in profusion can be seen and examined in the shops and demonstrations are often advertised.

The *Una* made by N.W. and Company and distributed by Atlas Sewing Machine Company in Camden Town, is a chain stitch machine date about 1870. *Courtesy Tolson Memorial Museum, Huddersfield*

The *Wanzer*. A modification, the *Little Wanzer* was advertised in *The Lady's Own Paper* of 1868. A lock stitch machine, it was priced at £4 4s. *Courtesy Tolson Memorial Museum, Huddersfield*

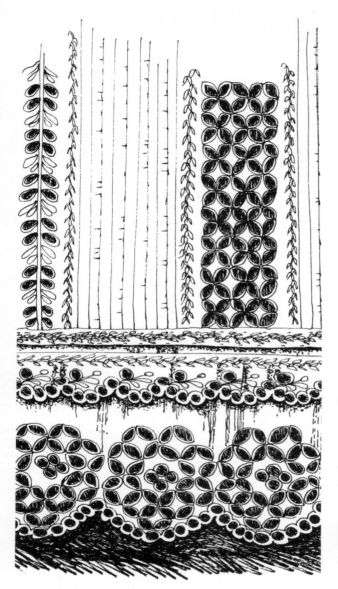

Part of the hand-worked front panel of a broderie anglaise Christening robe. It was the function of the nineteenth century multiple machines to reproduce this kind of embroidery as faithfully as possible

A petticoat flounce made on a multiple machine, imitating hand embroidery as closely as possible. It has a scalloped edge and a ribbon insert, both of which add to the cost of hand finishing

A spate of lavish 'fashion embroidery' erupted, once the full
potential of multiple machines was realised. These belt trimmings,
designed to emphasise an elegantly boned waistline, are
constructed on a soft tarlatan backing, with red, gold and yellow
silk and bronze metallic thread

A machine should be bought only after research, consultation and consideration. More and more zigzag machines are on the market and it is often very difficult to distinguish from brochures just what are the technical possibilities of a machine, even within the range of models in one particular brand. Commercial classification is both confusing and misleading. In the following pages machines are classified thus:

1 Straight stitch Basic straight sewing, no overedging or width to the stitch, the cheapest kind of machine.

2 Swing needle Straight sewing and zigzag stitching, overedging, satin stitch and buttonholing, but no variations.

3 Semi-automatic Straight sewing and zigzag stitching with some variations on the swing needle capabilities, like blind stitching.

4 Automatic Straight stitching and zigzag stitching, patterns which can be set and completed without further adjustments. The more sophisticated machines can reverse automatically to achieve complicated patterns, the most expensive kind of machine.

This book is designed for those who are already familiar with their machine, know how to care for it, and can competently control most sewing processes. Apart from the introduction and a little of the section on free machine stitchery technique, all the text is related directly to a photograph or drawing to facilitate closer comprehension of the illustrations. Once a basic grounding is achieved this layout should enable either student or teacher to approach new ideas without constant back reference, eventually adapting and recombining for more individual expression.

None of the techniques described here involves the purchase of any accessories other than those initially supplied with most semi-automatic machines. Eyelets, usually of 3·5 mm, 5 mm, and 6 mm diameter can be made automatically with added accessories, and there is a glide plate which fits under the presser foot for sewing friction surfaces like laminates and plastics.

Because fully automatic machines are a luxury, and because they add only a small and very dubious advantage to the possibilities of embroidery, their use is not discussed here.

An illustration from *Machine Embroidery, the artistic possibilities of the domestic sewing machine* by Dorothy Benson, published by the Singer Sewing Machine Company Ltd of London. A transparent wall panel worked in pastel organdies. *Courtesy of the Singer Company (UK) Ltd*

1 Embroidery with the presser foot

A prerequisite of rewarding machine embroidery is familiarity with the machine. Regular oiling, cleaning and simple maintenance are essential. The sewing machine brochures which claim immediate, easy success for everyone are very misleading. Anyone who has never used one before, either child or adult, needs a demonstration of how the straight stitch machine works. Then, after having completed some back-and-forth stitching with various stitch length adjustments to get the feel of speeds and control, the beginner should work through the manual or handbook step by step, far enough to become familiar with everything necessary for ordinary sewing, including thread tensions.

The next stage is to prepare some exercises in the form of drawn parallel or converging lines and varying curves, on either scrap paper or fabric, to be followed as accurately as possible with a machine-stitched line. These are manufactured (but available only in bulk) for use in training machinists in industry. Even the most experienced machinist, industrial, educational or domestic, needs a little practice with an unfamiliar make or specialised process before beginning a piece of work.

Children should not be sheltered from the frustrations of difficult materials for often these have the most exciting tactile or visual qualities. A great deal can be learned about fabric behaviour and possibilities from the simplest experiment. Overleaf, chamois leather is being applied to linen scrim with the Jones hand machine. This machine, sometimes known as the hourglass, has a long shuttle which runs on a horizontally fixed straight bar.

Fabric   evenweave linen
Thread   40 sewing thread
Tension   With top slightly slacker than spool, the same tension can be maintained throughout

The cotton football lace is sewn on with a short straight stitch. Run the machine very slowly so that the grain of the evenweave can be followed exactly. Accuracy can then be maintained by relating succeeding stitching to this first line. The plain zigzag near the bootlace is a short stitch, but not sufficiently close to produce a satin stitch. Two lengths of *Anchor Soft* hand embroidery cotton are twisted into a cord and couched down with a zigzag. On coarse, hard weaves the regularity of the stitch is distorted, so a long stitch is easier to control than a short one.

For table linen all the applied braids, threads and stitching should travel to the very edge of the fabric. They can then be finished off inside a hem or included in a frayed edge.

Some linens stretch if stitched with diagonal lines across the weave. This can usually be corrected by damping and stretching the finished piece. If the stitchery is to have more freedom than the example shown here, it would be best to back it with fine lawn before the embroidery is begun.

Simple border patterns are enlivened by slight variation, like the chevrons of the bootlace and the straight stitching, and the introduction of a secondary area of textural density like the one above the chevrons.

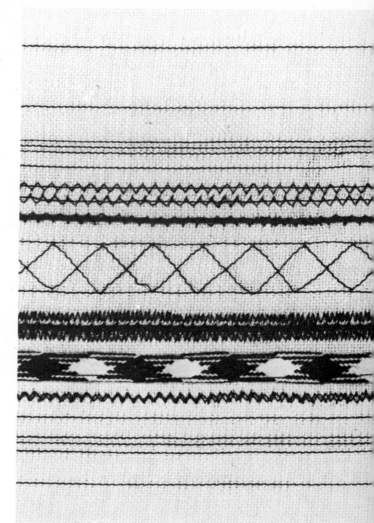

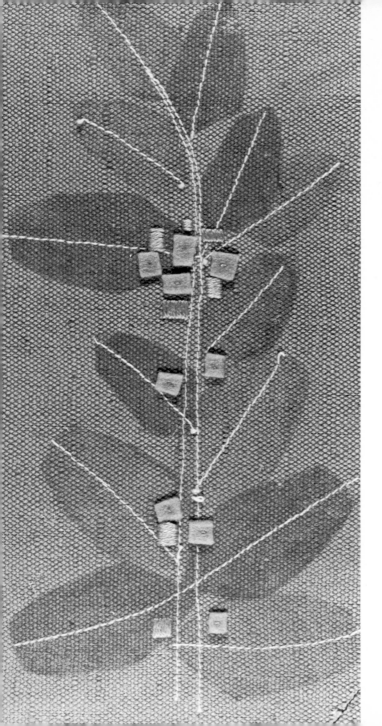

STRAIGHT STITCHING WITH THE PRESSER FOOT ON A PREPARED GROUND

Fabric cotton and rayon imitating linen
Thread 40 sewing thread
Tension an ordinary sewing stitch

A manilla coloured, closely woven, coarse fabric, potato printed with a soft orange dye. The white stitchery describes as simply as possible the main stem and leaf veins. Carefully considered squares of orange felt and white satin stitch applied by hand relieve the flatness. The needle is deviated from its path by the unyielding weave, making a beaded line. *Celia Wilson.*

Materials can be applied one to another on an elaborate scale and large areas can be worked with comparative ease. This Tahitian design lends itself particularly to appliqué. It could be worked in felts and other hard edged materials stitched down with a straight stitch, or luxuriant but fraying fabrics could be edged with satin stitch (very close zigzag), perhaps first backed with iron-on *Vilene*.

This kind of design, with natural divisions, can be worked in smaller pieces and then sewn together when all are completed.

In lighter fabrics it would make very beautiful curtaining, but it seems to demand a brash treatment in colourful, opaque fabric, of the sort which would make a blanket, wall hanging, rug or cape.

18

It is practical to work some kinds of patchwork with the machine. The obvious advantage is in the time factor, although care, accuracy and a certain amount of hand finishing are required.

This 305 mm (12 in.) square of log-cabin patchwork consists of a collection of old cotton prints chosen for their similarity of weight, body and behaviour. Many permutations of design are possible. In this case the darker fabrics are arranged on two sides only, leaving the other two quarters of the square for light and broken pattern. When the squares are joined side to side alternating diamonds of dark and light result. Another possibility is to work from dark at the extremities of the square to light in the middle, or vice versa, so making an illusion of undulating convex and concave forms when the squares are joined.

Cut a series of templates from thin card, progressing from a 50 mm (2 in.) square in 25 mm (1 in.) strips until a total area of 305 mm (12 in.) is reached. There are four similar strips at each progression, increased in length by 25 mm (1 in.) from their nearest inside neighbours. Iron the fabric and cut a strip to represent each template on the straight grain, leaving 10 mm (⅜ in.) seam allowance. Use some method of identification of the pieces, particularly if large quantities are to be cut at the same time.

Using a medium length straight stitch sew one of the shortest strips to the central square, stitching to exactly 10 mm (⅜ in.) from the edge of the square. Remove the sewing from the machine, leaving about 150 mm (6 in.) of thread attached to the material, and open out the seam. Add a second strip at right angles to the first, beginning stitching exactly where the first seam finished. Progress in this way until all four small strips are sewn to the square, then, using the ends of the threads, sew by hand each short seam which attaches one strip to another.

Repeat the process, each time treating the resulting square as the basis for the succeeding larger strips.

Tack each 305 mm (12 in.) square to a firm cotton backing of the same size and overlock the raw edges. Tack the squares so that corners match perfectly before sewing them together. Forty eight squares are needed for the top of a double bed. *Idea by Clair Wilson*

Two more forms of patchwork which are suitable for machine sewing. The one consisting of squares and rectangles can be used for varying materials, providing that those with a bias stretch are avoided. It is worked in long strips of pieces which then can be sewn together with a strong continuous seam. The diamond pattern is also made in strips. Here the grain of the fabric lies at 45° to the edge of each shape, but unless the fabric is very firm the grain should be parallel to the edges. This is particularly suitable for leather.

Fabric   white rayon velvet
Thread   50
Tension   both threads slightly slacker than ordinary sewing
Needle   80

Random lines of a metallic, flat, woven ribbon are stitched over the whole surface. The ribbon is fed to the front of the foot, held slightly at tension to keep it flat, thus puckering the velvet which runs beneath the presser foot considerably faster. Because the stitched line cannot be kept central on the ribbon its angled reflection is more emphasised. This process stiffens the fabric and causes it to roll, so that its characteristics are considerably changed. It could be used for bodices, where the body would support its shape, or for garments with a stiff lining, or for millinery.

It is capable of many variations, both with and without the presser foot. With the darning foot and a wide zigzag it is one of the few techniques possible on stretch fabrics. Because of its ease and speed it is particularly suitable for theatrical costume, quickly giving an opulent appearance. $\frac{3}{4}$ actual size.

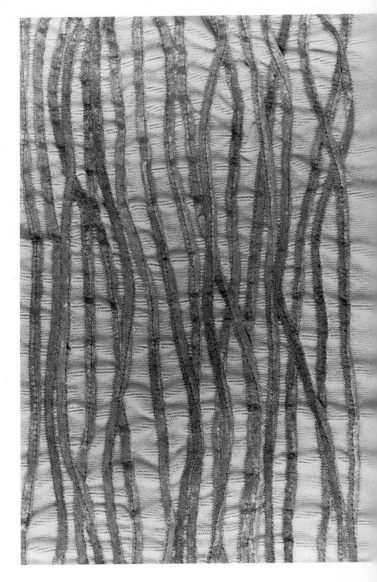

Two stocking or miser purses worked on rectangles of soft, thin fabric about 305 mm long × 150 mm (12 in. × 6 in.) wide. Ribbons, braids, lace and strips of fabric are applied across the shorter measurement to give rich texture and subtle colour, leaving the central portion plain. The rectangle is then seamed to make a long cylinder and lined, leaving a central slit which must be hand finished. Old brass curtain rings are used for closures. On one of the purses these have been button-holed with plastic raffia. For variety, one end is bunched and finished with a tassel whilst the other is flat and beaded. The coins are contained in the ends while the purse is carried either in the hand or over the belt by the central portion with the opening. The rings slide to give access to the money.

Embroidery is an activity which demands acquisitiveness. A wealth of available material, in the wider sense of the word, brings richness to both colour and textural variation. Improvisation and resourcefulness introduce an element of chance, so alleviating a tendency for overdeliberation. ⅔ actual size.

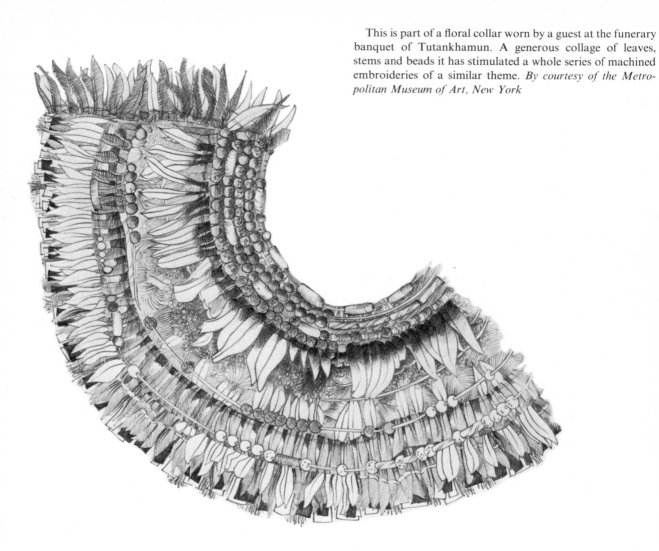

This is part of a floral collar worn by a guest at the funerary banquet of Tutankhamun. A generous collage of leaves, stems and beads it has stimulated a whole series of machined embroideries of a similar theme. *By courtesy of the Metropolitan Museum of Art, New York*

A shoulder bag based on the design of the Tutankhamun collar. A long rectangle of stout fabric forms both sides and base, completely covered by other fabrics in soft greens and warm blues. The pale piece at the top is a batik-dyed cotton with felt shapes applied, the results of cutting the strip of felt immediately below. Each frayed edge is sewn behind the next piece, in this case a fine silk liberally criss-crossed with zigzag. Scraps of felt and wired tassels are sewn firmly under the felt. A shaded tatting border, a jumble sale find, embellishes a flat ribbon, and they are both sewn down at the same time as some pointed tubes of fine wool and satin. These are made independently and sewn with their seams uppermost. They require a surprisingly large area of fabric. Cutting them across the grain can make them fall in soft spirals, especially with some stretchy fabrics. Another layer of tubes lies beneath, bordered by a pale satin. The base of the bag has thick lengths of a bulky upholstery fringing. Strap and zip top are made separately, and the whole thing lined.

Collages of this kind grow from a mound of bits selected for their colour. Further selectivity occurs as the piece progresses, choice being determined by what has gone before and by the size of the scraps. The other side of the bag is in the same colour range but is quite different.

Those shown in colour plate 1, facing page 32, are made with acetate rayons.

Choose a piece of dark lustrous fabric, iron it perfectly flat and back it with iron-on *Vilene*. Cut a rectangle 280 mm × 100 mm plus 10 mm (11 in. × 4 in. plus ⅜ in.) all round for a seam allowance. Apply varying stripes of paler fabrics to imitate a humbug structure, limiting the colour and selecting only those with a reflective quality. Take care to achieve a straight grain, flatness and even stitchery. Seam A to A to form a cylinder. Fold at B and C, seam, and turn right side out.

Use soft, resilient stuffing like *dacron*, *terylene* or *kapok*. Fold at D and E, turn in the seam allowance and hand stitch.

On a larger scale this idea makes exciting cushions, but the sugary allusions are only maintained crisply if the humbugs remain non functional.

Each individual colour is changed by those which juxtapose, superimpose or reflect onto it. Even the softest colours can introduce a complementary contrast or receive the characteristics of their neighbours. Thus, unless colour choice is backed by a sound knowledge of the probabilities it is best to test the results on scraps of waste fabric first. (See also colour plate 1, facing page 32).

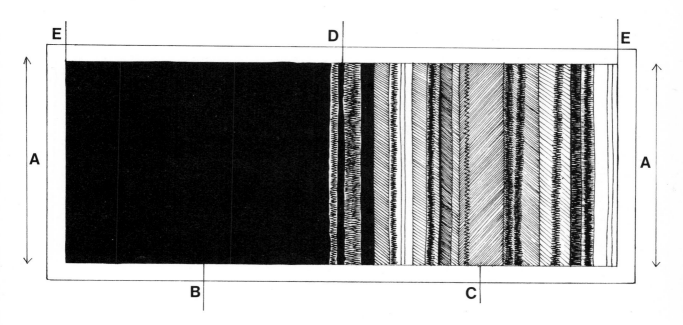

Stump work is the over indulged three dimensional embroidery of the fifteenth to the seventeenth centuries which is raised from the surface of the fabric by stumps of wood or padding. The Victorians, too, enjoyed this indulgence, using wools, beads, raffia, bisque and wax. It is a technique particularly suitable for lightweight synthetics. The drawing is a detail from an embroidered panel in soft blues and silver on the theme of flower pieces in glass domes. The diagram shows how the 'lay' of the flower can be arranged on two layers of rayon acetate or silk tacked together, each petal being machined with a narrow zigzag through both layers,

leaving very small turnings. The inner point of each petal must be left open for turning and stuffing. It need not be hand finished as this part is hidden. The shaded petal shapes on the diagram are not included in the flower shown, but indicate that tiny petals could be used instead of the centre. When all the petals are completed they are layered together at the inner points with a strong thread and sewn firmly into their beds of leaves, buds and stems. The centre is a large wooden bead closely buttonholed with pale blue plastic raffia. The wire and nylon butterflies are confectionery decorations.

2 Free machine embroidery

A few tools are needed for free machine embroidery, together with the right threads and needles. A darning foot is not necessary.

1 A cover for the feed dog on the few machines where this is needed. Cover plates can be difficult to find. An alternative is to raise the level of the throat plate with metal washers placed between the plate and the screw holes, so that the feed dog is no longer in contact with the fabric.

2 An adjustable tambour frame, metal, wood or plastic, is essential to progress at all.

3 Machine embroidery threads which are finer and more pliable than sewing threads. Sewing cotton (40) can still be used for coarse work, but this is extravagant. Embroidery threads can be very fine, but 50 is the most available and popular. Thicker yarns of a considerable range can be used in the spool, but for early practice, 50s in both needle and spool are best. It is well worth hunting for any fine machining threads and experimenting with different fabrics, stitches and tensions.

4 Fine needles. For practising or for coarse work, a number 90 needle is suitable, the one used for most sewing purposes. A number 80 is best for the more competent and for general purposes. A 70 is the correct size for very delicate work.

5 A very small screwdriver, which is supplied as an accessory with modern machines.

6 A plentiful supply of spools, stored end to end in a flat box so that their contents show.

Joe is using a Duiselmann treadle with a long hook and boat shaped shuttle to practice direction and speed control. Like all treadles without a motor it is liable to reverse at stopping and starting and is therefore difficult to control for very delicate stitchery. However, it produces a good, regular lock stitch and is still in use for heavier work.

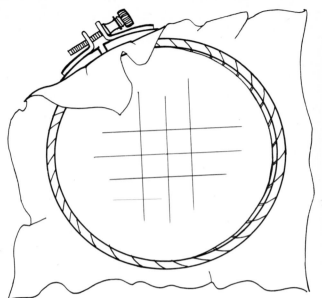

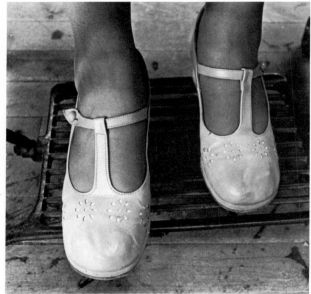

Set up the sewing machine in a well lit area on an even floor surface and a firm working surface. Choose a chair at a comfortable height and place the foot control within easy reach. On an electrically driven treadle more precise control results with one foot placed forward from the other, the toes of one to accelerate and the heel of the other to slow down. A portable flat-bed or free-arm machine has its sewing surface raised above table level so that the hands are less comfortable. One solution is to place the machine well back on the table and put a block of wood or firm 'sausage' of fabric in front of the machine to bring arms and hands back to the same level. This idea may involve substituting a higher chair. Comfort, without hunching or eyestrain, is essential.

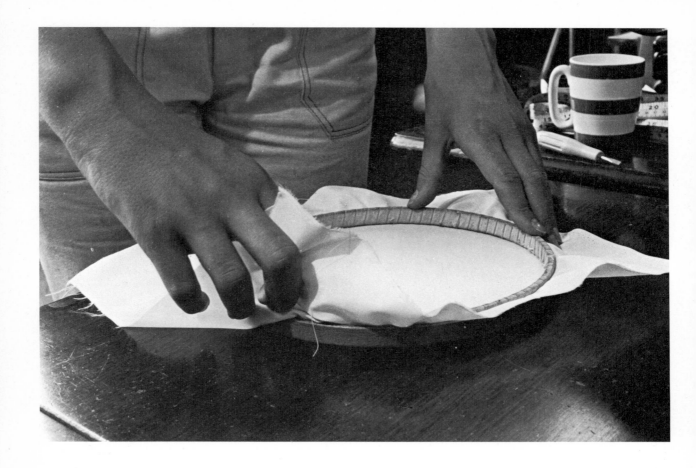

Wind machine embroidery cotton 50 onto the spool and thread the needle with the same gauge in another colour. This idea will help to show the characteristics of stitch tension and can be discarded as soon as these are understood. Check by testing on a piece of scrap fabric that the machine is producing a good sewing stitch. In free embroidery this is referred to as darning stitch. Needle thread and spool thread interlock within the thickness of the fabric so that neither is visible on its opposing side.

Raise the presser foot lever and remove the presser foot and its screw. Lower the feed dog or cover it with a plate. These actions prevent the ordinary sewing process of the feed dog rotating against the presser foot and so leave control to the embroiderer.

Select a piece of scrap cotton material, something plain, evenly textured, firm and fairly closely woven, and stretch it evenly and tightly in a tambour frame. This is worth doing well.

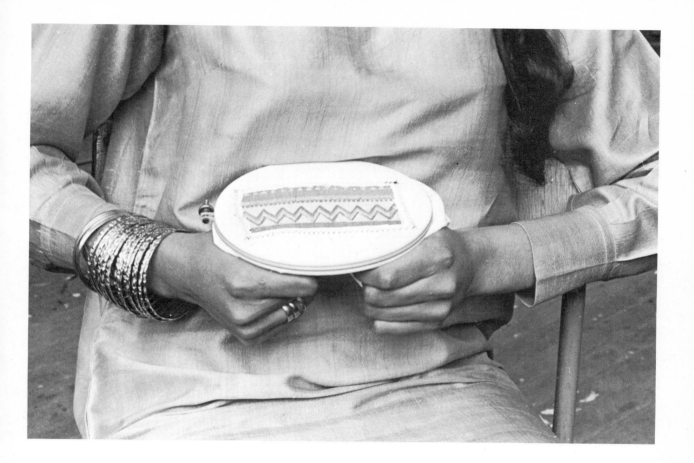

On a wooden or plastic frame the inner ring should be firmly bound with soft tape to prevent the fabric slipping, and set slightly lower than the outer one, so that the wrong side of the material will be in contact with the throat plate of the machine. On a metal frame the outer ring, which is circular in section, can be bound. The grain of the fabric must be really tight and not distorted. If this process damages the fabric then it is not sufficiently closely woven for practicing purposes. A small tambour frame is best to begin, of 140 mm (5½ in.) or less inside diameter.

The operation of stretching the fabric correctly is made easier by placing both frame and fabric on an uncluttered, flat surface. A metal frame is particularly strong and will withstand the strain of considerable stretching and tightening to the extent that a percussive note can be made by tapping the fabric.

Raise the needle to its highest point and carefully slip the stretched fabric underneath it. Lower the presser foot lever to engage top tension and take one stitch through the fabric with the hand wheel to bring up the spool thread. Holding the ends of both threads between fingers and frame, and controlling the frame lightly with thumb and second finger on either side, make some long, slow verticals and horizontals.

PLATE I   Humbugs made of acetate rayons and stuffed with dacron. Individual colours are changed by those which juxtapose, superimpose or reflect onto them. Actual size 500 mm (20 in.) deep. (See also page 25)

32

The extent of the work is governed by the sides of the tambour frame, particularly at the back where the presser bar will prevent the needle travelling right to the edge. This can be seen clearly here in a first piece on brushed cotton by a young adult. The stitchery tentatively explores the confines afforded by the frame and in so doing forcibly relates the personal to the mechanical. Once a regular speed can be maintained the normal vibrations of the machine can be utilised to encourage a flow which is sensitive to the characteristics of the fabric.

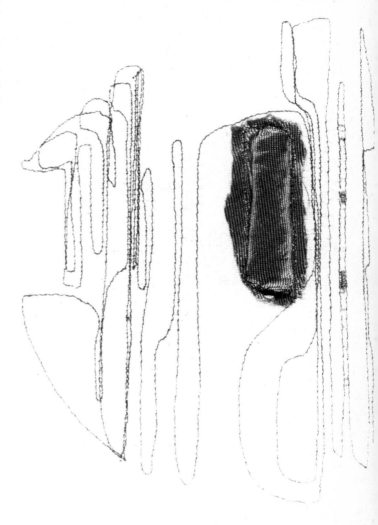

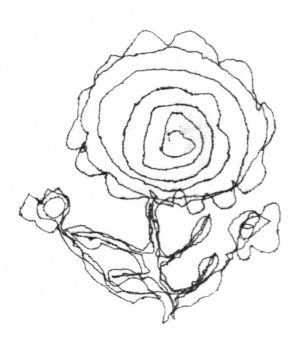

Two more first attempts, chosen to show the minimal difference in control distinguishable in the earliest stage. The first, on white seersucker, is by a nine year old boy, the second, on terylene, is by a seventeen year old girl. This simple motif seems to be spontaneous and universal.

Find those movements which feel most difficult and practice them. Concentrate on regulating the speed of the machine in relation to the speed of the hands until both are controllable.

If the machine is refusing to stitch, check that
The needle is correctly set
The needle is correctly threaded
There is no obstruction between throat plate and fabric
The frame is stretched firmly with warp and weft threads at
    right angles to each other.
If the thread is continually breaking check that
The presser foot is lowered
The needle is sharp and not too fine for the thread
The stitches attempted are not too long
The stitches are not too concentrated in one place
The machine is not overburdened with heavy fabrics
The needle is travelling centrally through its hole in the throat
    plate
The needle hole in the throat plate is smooth and undamaged.

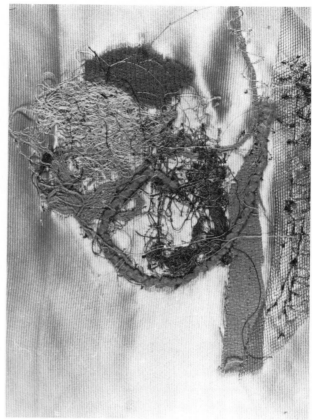

Once the feel of moving the surface under the needle has been experienced another start will produce more controlled results. These two examples, besides indicating two quite different personalities, show that there can be varying responses to the problem of control. The precise, floral one on rayon acetate in pinks and purples, is by a student who is already an accomplished machinist and has experience in a variety of hand embroidery techniques. She has used 50 in the needle and 40 in the spool and experimented with varying both tensions. × ½ actual size.

The informal one, by an inexperienced student gifted with curiosity, investigates on a simulated ribbed silk the textural possibilities of collage pieces immediately to hand, collecting wools and yarns in reds and ochres. Collage is perhaps best avoided at this stage, mainly because of the danger to fingers close to the needle, but its visual and tactile excitement cannot be suppressed for long. During these early stages there is a tendency to bring the fingers nearer and nearer to the needle, to achieve more precise control. Experienced machine embroiderers steer alarmingly close to their fingers, and real initiation occurs only when the index finger is well and truly impaled. × ⅔ actual size.

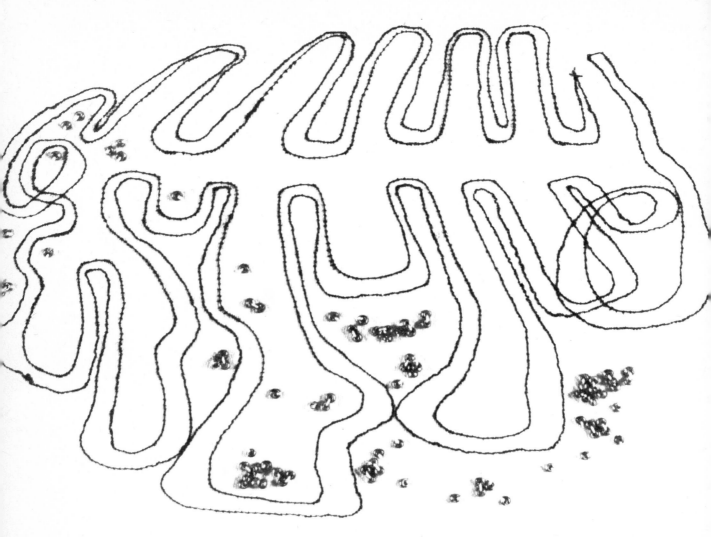

Fabric firm rayon with diagonal weave
Thread 50

This pattern is derived from a drawing of muck-spreading journeys across a rough pasture high in the Yorkshire Dales. The grass is cropped velvet short by the sheep in the early spring, and the lines left by the tractor describe the exact shape of the humps and hollows. Even a slight slope will distort the equality of the lines as they converge, and the

necessity of turning a tractor on relatively level ground flattens each curve. The boulders are represented by clumps of dull beads sewn on by hand.

Remember that it is practical and characteristic to make continuous lines. Any attempts to draw the patterns previously will soon be abandoned as futile; too much deliberation can be destructive.

Fabric   heavy furnishing cotton in white with a mercerised weft

Thread   50

A ribbed lurex silk has been padded with soft foam rubber and sewn down under a layer of net with several lines of stitchery. The net protects the raw edge of the silk and is cut away afterwards over the central cushion. A gap is left, to be finished later with a hand couched thread of jap gold, and an outer circle supports linear stitchery in direct contrast to the solidarity of the applied piece. The french knots are hand stitched. This kind of stitchery will withstand wear and friction and, with the exception of the gold thread, will wash repeatedly.

A fund of decorative clichés is soon amassed and journeys into the desert of fabric become more self confident. Machine embroidery produces a plethora of comfortable circular motifs because these are the easiest to use as practice pieces. Unlike mass produced embroidery, pattern cannot be exactly repeated, speed and judgement never being quite coordinated, and thus free machine stitching acquires its recognisable characteristics.

Stop the machine and turn the tambour frame round a few degrees occasionally, so that there is no set orientation. This will help to discover the most successful direction in which to 'draw' a particular kind of line. Curves, for instance, are most fluid when the wrist is in the position of axis, so turn the frame so that the inside of the curve is nearest the thumbs.

Confidence and control will be accelerated by frequent practice at first, one evening class per week is not sufficient.

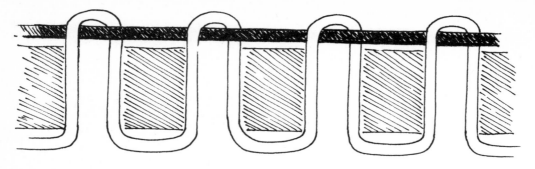

Whip stitch

Darning stitch

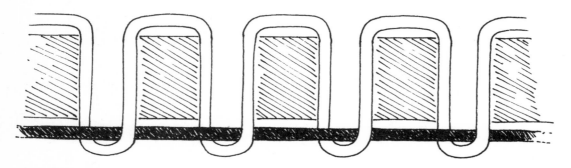

Cable stitch

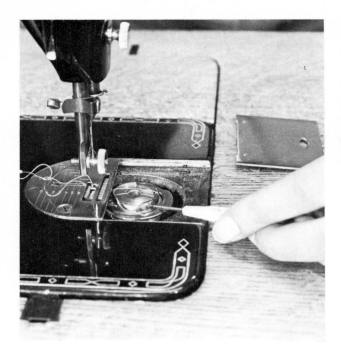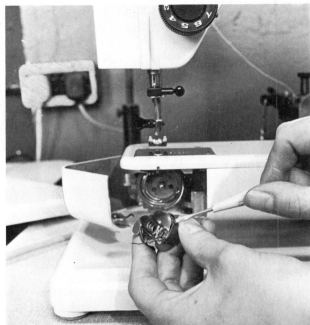

Unlike hand embroidery, which has the wealthy vocabulary of traditional and ethnic variation in stitchery, machine embroidery can boast only four stitches. These are achieved by varying the relationship between needle and spool thread tension. At this stage the idea of using a different colour in the spool will be appreciated.

Darning stitch has already been described on page 30, and it is shown in the centre of these sectional diagrams. Now that the presser foot is removed and the fabric is stretched in the frame any slight discrepancy will be accentuated, so adjustments may be necessary. Adjustment of the spool tension is less familiar than that of the top tension but just as simple. There are two small screws on the spool casing, one securing the tension spring and the other a short way along it. The second one needs a turn of only a few degrees to change spool tension considerably. It is a small grub screw, easily removed and lost and not so easy to replace, so care should be taken particularly when loosening it.

WHIP STITCH

Fabric loosely woven rayon acetate
Thread 50

Whip stitch produces a quite different kind of line, one that is capable of considerable variation. The lower tension must be loosened so that the spool thread is pulled up onto the surface of the fabric.

The illustration shows at the top left the spool thread loosened just a little, so that it appears as regularly spaced dots along the needle thread. It has then been made progressively looser, each time making two experimental areas of stitchery, the top one moving the frame faster so that the stitches are wide apart, and beneath this moving the frame slower so that the stitches are close.

40 sewing cotton for both needle and spool thread produces a heavy whip stitch, but this cannot be an accentuated one because the spool thread is too thick to be collected in long loops. With the usual 50 thread on the spool and a 40 in the needle the stitches can be placed closely to form a fine cord. With the threads reversed a tortuous line results from compacting the thick spool loops.

A firm, regular whip stitch can be achieved with a monofilament thread in the needle and a 50 on the spool. This combination also produces an exciting feather stitch (discussed opposite), where the needle thread is invisible except for a slight gleam. It is well worth finishing off monofilament thread by hand. × 2 actual size.

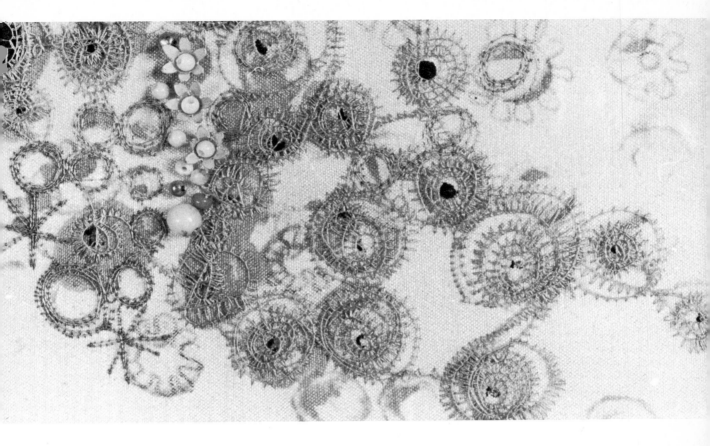

FEATHER STITCH

Fabric   pale cream rayon acetate imitating hand woven silk,
hand printed in grey
Thread   50

By tightening the top tension and loosening the spool so
that the difference is highly exaggerated, the variations of
whip stitch can be extended into what is often referred to as
feather stitch. Continuous curving produces the most interesting results, the tight needle thread describing a concentric
circle much smaller than the path of the needle. If the strain on
the top thread leads to breaking decrease the tension slightly
so that an attractive stitch results without this inconvenience.
This is a detail from plate 3, facing page 64. × 2 actual size.

CABLE STITCH

Fabric   loosely woven rayon acetate
Thread   needle 50, a variety of gauges on the spool

Some thicker threads can only be accommodated on the spool, and if they will not pass behind the slackened tension spring easily they can be run off the spool directly, relying on their own tension. For cable stitch the top tension must be slackened to produce what can best be described as an upside-down whip stitch, and the right side of the work is that which is in contact with the throat plate. The stitchery is done from the wrong side. At this stage it will be better to use similar colours top and bottom to appreciate the textures of lines made by varying threads rather than the quality of the stitch. Usually the heavy thread lies on the surface couched down by the thinner thread from the needle, but if top tension is tightened slightly a more broken line appears, rather like little beads.

For the illustration a variety of threads are used. Linen machine thread 40 produces a hard, clean line. *Coton à broder* is shiny but more elastic, pulling larger loops from the needle.

Floss silk is softly twisted, creates a more flattened ridge and reflects the light beautifully as it changes direction. Stranded embroidery cotton has less reflection, and because it flows from the spool easily, creates a slightly beaded effect. The individual strands tend to catch on the needle's downward journey, making a rougher line. Tapestry wool leaves the spool with difficulty, so pulling long loops from the needle thread and producing a slightly quilted effect as it bunches the weft threads of the fabric.

Always pull the spool thread through the fabric before beginning to stitch. The design should produce a continuous line because finishing off must be done by hand. Always check first on a trial piece that the tension, thread and stitch length are exactly what is required. This stitching can be interesting applied more rigidly under the presser foot.

On those machines which will take a thick thread through a large needle the effect of cable stitching, technically a whip stitch, can be achieved on a small scale right way up.

3 Technical developments

Machine embroidery is at its most useful for permanent marking and labelling. The *Marbles* bag was worked in a frame before the bag was sewn, with a 50 cotton in an orange zigzag on blue wool. Lettering can be planned briefly beforehand with a chinagraph pencil or tailor's chalk, but overdeliberation denies the characteristics of the machine stitching. Thicks and thins are determined by the angle of the stitch in relation to the letterforms. A similar angle should be maintained throughout unless block letters in satin stitch are required.

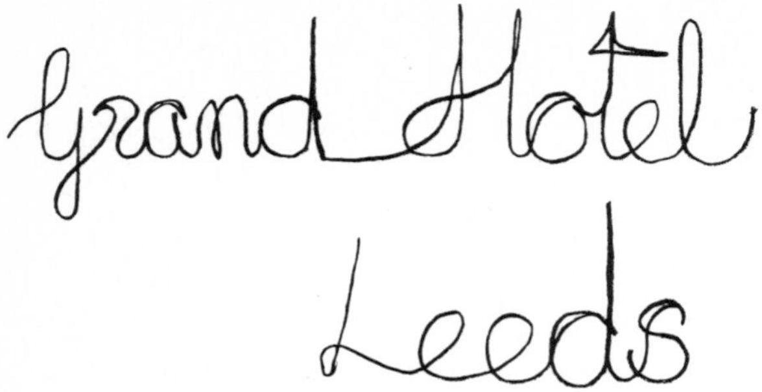

Grand Hotel Leeds

The Infirmary Wakefield

Perhaps the earliest functional use of free hand machine embroidery was the labelling of linen in hotels and hospitals, which is now being superseded by indelible markers. Domestics whose whole occupation is taken up with this can still be found in larger hospitals. They use a treadle or an electric machine, a darning foot or a frame, a straight stitch or a zigzag. The pantograph, a jointed framework of rods based on the geometry of a parallelogram, is sometimes still used for copying the lines of an original drawing.

Design is a complex of attitudes and ideas strongly influenced by creative climate and personality. Sources are everywhere and anywhere, visual, tangible, audible and emotional. Techniques stimulate ideas and ideas find an appropriate technique. In a book of this kind dealing with a specific medium, sources of design can merely be hinted at, and at best give a channelled, personal viewpoint. Working with children encourages an immediacy and directness of expression which can be either naive or sophisticated, and is not easy to achieve in a slow, deliberate medium like embroidery. Young childrens' lack of social inhibition allows of a freedom lost by most adults, a freedom which shows clearly in these tree drawings. Their original colours and media made them unsuitable for reproduction but they have been redrawn as faithfully as possible. They all lend themselves to collage and linear stitchery, probably because of an unconscious influence from surrounding activities.

FREE ZIGZAG IN THE FRAME

Fabric   loosely woven acetate rayon
Thread   50
Tension   top tension slackened to form the stitch loop on the wrong side of the fabric
Needle   90

The warp (vertical) of this fabric consists of a continuous filament thread with very little crimp, which creates an obstacle for the needle and therefore distorts the stitched line. The soft, bulky weft allows the machine thread to sink, making an indeterminate line. On the left is a darning stitch, looping because the top tension is slack, and then the width of the stitch is progressively increased. The machine is maintained at the same speed throughout, but the movement of the frame is speeded up for the spread zigzag and slowed down for the close satin stitch.

MORE CONTROL WITH ZIGZAG STITCHING IN THE FRAME

Fabric　firm rayon with diagonal weave
Thread　50
Tension　top tension slackened to form the stitch loop on the wrong side of the fabric, top tension tightened for understated whip stitch
Needle　90

This is derived from a drawing of limestone escarpments. Volcanic action has up-ended the strata where the glaciers and the climate have eroded it into massive, precarious blocks, overhanging scree slopes.

With the zigzag set to its widest for the blocks of stone, the stitching can be begun in each case with an unobtrusive line of straight stitching and finished in the same way. The whole is completed in one journey, the frame being turned sometimes for the varying lean of the stones. Greater width can be built up by overlapping there-and-back journeys. The top tension is then tightened slightly to produce a very flat whip stitch for the wiggling texture, and tightened yet again for the more open line beneath, where the frame has been moved much faster to produce widely spaced stitches.

ZIGZAG ON THE STRAIGHT STITCH MACHINE IN A FRAME

Fabric nylon chiffon, white seersucker, a cotton floral print and pale pink jap silk over cobalt blue cheese cloth

Thread 50, soft orange in the needle and deep blue on the spool

Tension both very slack, with the blue spool thread sometimes showing at the extremity of the stitch

Needle 80, for the delicacy of the fabrics but the strength to resist the side pull

This is the only kind of zigzag which can be made with a straight stitch machine. It must be done on a tightly stretched frame and is achieved by moving the frame violently from side to side in rhythm with the needle, so that just one stitch is taken on alternate sides of the zigzag. It shows here as a much rougher texture than that of the mechanical zigzag or the horizontal hand stitching. Although it is difficult to control at first a little practice will make it a favourite. Used as a cable stitch (worked upside-down with a thick thread in the spool), it is capable of exciting variation.

This is a detail of the panel on page 62. Actual size.

CLOSE WHIP STITCH TEXTURES IN THE FRAME

Fabric greenish buff satin

Thread 50, pale blue in the needle and a darker green on the spool

Tension a tight needle thread and a slack spool thread

Needle 90

Whip stitch can be built up to make an almost impenetrable texture. Here its matt surface contrasts with the satin, and the hardness of the whole is emphasised by mounting it onto thin card before stitching it to the ground. The fabric is cut to the shape of the card leaving small turnings and then glued on the wrong side only. The technique of working separate areas and applying them afterwards is a useful one.

This is another detail of the panel on page 62. $\times \frac{2}{3}$ actual size.

Fabric natural soft cotton cambric ground, painted with very pale lilac brush strokes, with an applied blue rayon repp with alternating stripes of twill and slub
Thread silver lurex, purple sewing 40, brown embroidery 30
Tension top slackened for firm zigzag and even tensions for the lurex
Needle 70

This detail from a landscape panel by Celia Wilson shows a flat rock face and the moon represented as a hole in the sky.

All the stitchery is done with a presser foot and without a frame. The repp is applied with a zigzag which frays its curves. Brown and deep lilac wools are couched with an open zigzag and one fine darning wool is couched by hand. Three short lengths of chain stitch are also by hand. The stitch length consistency over the pale area cannot be achieved without the presser foot. Stitch width is varied, and occasional discrepancies in the continuity of line are used to describe faults in the strata. A long darning stitch running in the general direction of the weft sinks between the threads making a very fine line. The lurex thread was applied from the spool with the wrong side of the work uppermost and even tensions.

Spools should always be filled evenly. Some machines need a little manual assistance with this. Lurex must be guided on by hand so that it lies flat, its own spool revolving on a pencil held a short distance from the bobbin spindle. Because it has no elasticity it need not pass through the spool thread tension device.

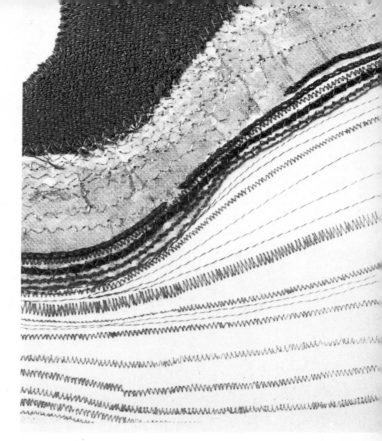

PLATE 2 Sometimes machine embroidery functions merely as a convenient sewing down and softening process as a basis for heavier collage. On this little panel, designed specifically for the silver frame, the machining is scarcely visible but much more practical than hand stitchery. The figures are printed as paper cut-outs and are here mounted on *Vilene* and slightly padded

ZIGZAG AND TENSION CHANGES

Fabric rag bag scraps of purple cotton poplin applied to purple and black wool bouclé
Thread sewing 40
Tension varied
Needle 90

This is another detail from a panel by Celia Wilson, a landscape with earth and field patterns.

The shapes are sewn down first by hand with a small running stitch and all the machine stitching is done with the presser foot. Because there is black thread in the needle and white on the spool, this example demonstrates clearly the versatility of zigzag stitching. Apart from stitch width and length variations, and qualities of lines achieved by couching, tension changes can produce another set of permutations. At bottom right is an area of texture made by increasing the top tension so that the spool thread is looped up to join the narrowing pattern made by the needle thread, while in other places the white spool cotton appears less obtrusively.

Free machine embroidery lends itself to an incessant flow of small rounded motifs. Both these are practical for dress purposes and will withstand hard wear and frequent washing. The one on a blue flecked creamy silk has a navy satin cushion applied with several rows of darning stitch over a circle of wadding. The stitching is done through a larger circle of net which controls the fraying edge of the satin and can be cut away over the cushion afterwards. The outside edge of the net is beneath the satin stitch. The flecks on the ground are brought into the motif directly with stitchery, and it is finished with hand chain stitch and beads.

The second motif has a ground of cotton with warm coloured stripes, and the emerald green rayon cushion is applied under chiffon. The embroidery is white and cream and the beads of kingfisher colours. On the first motif the zigzag circle is worked with the frame facing one way only, but on the second the frame is turned so that the stitch radiates. $\times 1\frac{1}{2}$ actual size.

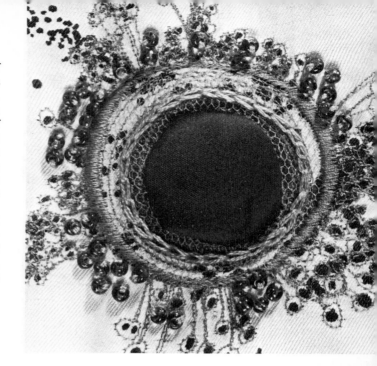

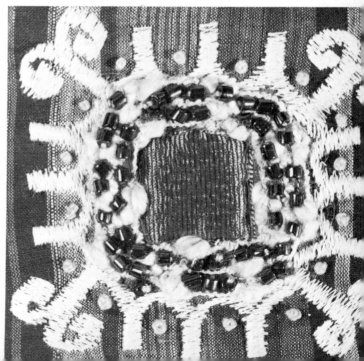

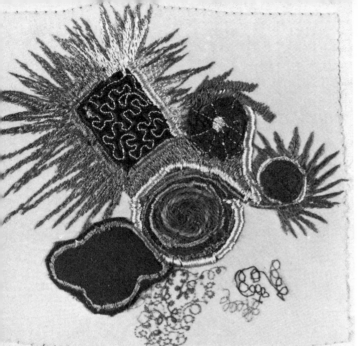

SATIN STITCH IN THE FRAME

There are as many approaches to the use of machine stitchery as there are machine stitchers. Two small extended motifs by Tajinder Saund introduce many fresh elements and at the same time draw upon the richness of an Indian tradition. The vigorous one is in purple, pink and orange yarns and stitchery, applying small pieces of cotton and lining material. Yarns are coiled and applied with radiating darning stitch. The solid satin stitch is mainly in a rayon thread, travelling in whichever direction seems to be appropriate at the moment of working. The imitation of hand embroidered long and short stitch seems quite appropriate in this context.

The floral one on a cream cambric ground uses shaded machine 50 in red, orange and green primaries bordered with hand stitchery. All the solidity is achieved with stitchery. The open flower is edged with shaded satin stitch over a cord, and the ground is embellished with what was once called 'granite stitch'. This kind of stitchery is more durable than the fabric which supports it, and so its uses are limitless.

The undulating quality of this design owes its origins to two things; a series of studies of frilly seaweeds, and some experiments with collections of coloured crayons and felt tipped pens bunched in lavish fistfuls. The scale of machine zigzag will only allow of an interpretation about 250 mm (10 in.) in length, and so the design would be ideal for collars and cuffs or extending into a border. Undulating zigzag can be interesting on a ribbed silk ground where the fabric texture distorts the direction of the line.

A wood boring beetle tunnels these workings, the larvae fattening in their individual galleries. There are industrial single head machines whose zigzag width can be graduated with a knee control, but on domestic machines this must be done with the right hand. Smoothly shaded satin stitch is achieved by framing the ground and using a presser foot, so that the right hand is free to adjust the stitch width lever.

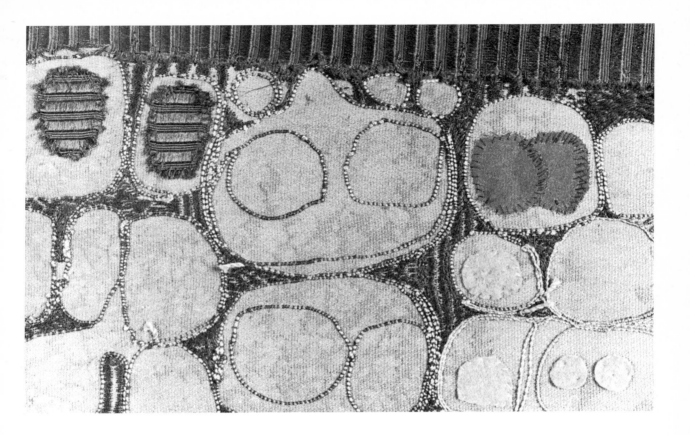

CABLE STITCH IN THE FRAME

Fabric heavy, deep navy, ribbed satin on khaki rayon/cotton with a subdued amber print
Thread black 40 sewing cotton in the needle, pale lilac *coton à broder* on the spool
Tension needle thread tight, spool thread outside the tension spring

Remember that cable stitch is worked from the wrong side of the material. Its richness is obvious in this detail from a landscape by Celia Wilson. The ribbed satin frays quickly, so it is applied with some hand stitchery first, and then its tasselled edge is made a prominent textural feature. A variety of line is achieved by the spacing of the machine stitches and by recognition of the fact that tension changes occur with direction changes.

This detail shows an experienced knowledge of the relative scale of stitchery. The coarse treatment of cable stitch and some applied pieces is in keeping with a large panel, and yet there is delicate hand stitchery with satin stitch blocks, french and bullion knots and seeding, all used with a patient sympathy for natural qualities. Because embroidery is an over-deliberate medium many stitchers develop little idiosyncratic trade marks, intentional accidents, like the unfinished ends of the cable stitch easily visible here. Actual size.

4 Transferring designs and some working methods

There is some controversy about the process of transferring designs from paper to fabric, and it is misleading to insist upon a correct method for each particular fabric or technique. For this reason the preparation of several quite different pieces of work is described in this chapter in an attempt to cover most of the possibilities. Ambitious pieces require consideration beforehand and some time set aside for the transferring process, and sometimes it is even worth making a work study list.

Carbon paper should be used only after experienced deliberation.

This drawing of an intended appliqué is accompanied by a diagram showing how its main shapes could be indicated on the fabric with hand stitchery or a fine, hard pencil line. With the main shapes indicated only by very basic dots the machine is allowed its role as an independent medium. For a fine, pale fabric the design could be traced directly, or for thicker, darker grounds the drawing could be cut into jigsaw pieces and delicately drawn round with a chinagraph pencil. For a thick or pile fabric the design could be traced onto tissue paper and tacked through, the tissue being torn away afterwards.

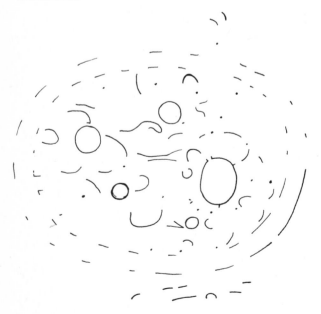

CUTTING UP A CARTOON

The drawing is derived from an opened out paper bag interior in which some dyed beans have been left to dry. The dye colours have absorbed into the paper at varying rates, leaving a myriad of soft and hard edges. Its fluid lines make it very suitable for machine stitchery on a large scale.

For big panels, wall hangings or rugs it is more likely that changes in design may be made during the working process, and therefore a flexible transferring method is preferable. All designs which are to be enlarged or reduced should be squared-up, ie both design and ground fabric divided into equal and corresponding sub-divisions, so that accuracy can be constantly checked. The design can be divided directly with a fine pencil line or on an overlay of tracing paper or transparent film, and the fabric can be squared with tacking lines. By enclosing the original design with a rectangle the new dimensions can easily be determined if one measurement is known.

In this case the design was squared up with an overlay, and copied onto a corresponding series of enlarged rectangles of the same proportion drawn out on large sheets of brown paper. The ground fabric was marked with the squares and suspended from a wood batten, and then the full size cartoon was cut up, each piece being pinned to the ground fabric in its turn and drawn round with tailor's chalk. In this way the squaring up divisions of both cartoon and ground fabric can be constantly checked for alignment.

Most of the stitching was done without a frame, using mainly the darning foot, or couching yarns, braids and narrow ribbons with the braiding foot.

PRICK AND POUNCE

A detail from a late *art nouveau* hand embroidery is used in the form of an appliqué for the upholstered back of a nursing chair.

The drawing was enlarged onto strong, thin paper by the squaring-up method, its proportions also being changed at this stage by making a slightly more squat rectangle and adapting the smaller squares proportionately. An uneven distribution in relation to the centre line was also adjusted as the full size drawing progressed. Accurate measurement was essential, checking the positions of shapes in relation to the rectangles in each case. The cartoon was then placed in the position of the intended embroidery to check scale, proportion and balance. The allowance of fabric required beyond the edge of the rectangle was noted in numerals at each side of the cartoon.

The paper was turned upside down over a padded surface and the lines of the design perforated with a needle, sufficiently closely to describe detail. The velvet ground was pressed on a velvet board (a miniature bed of nails which accommodate the pile whilst the fabric is ironed on the back), and smoothed evenly on a hard surface. Pinning was not necessary and could distort the grain. The cartoon was placed right way up on the fabric and then, because decisions about the design were finalised, a mixture of oil paint and turps, somewhat lighter in colour than the ground, was rubbed through sparingly with a hog hair brush. The usual medium is pounce (powdered chalk or charcoal and chalk), but pounce is intended merely to mark a line which is subsequently painted with poster colour, and velvet and many other pile fabrics are impossible to paint. Oil bound paints cannot be removed, so the pricked line, which must be accurate, is the sole guide. Both media are used in industry and in either case the pricked cartoon can be re-used with no loss of detail.

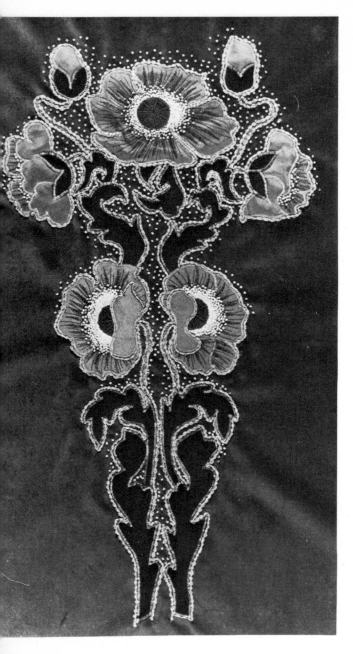

The design for the chair back was now transferred to the fabric and a means must be found to apply the leaves and flowers. The ground was a deep, soft pink and the leaves were an equally subtle blue. Flowers and buds were a blue-purple satin.

All the applied fabrics were pressed and backed with iron-on *Vilene*. The satin for the flowers was stretched in a large tambour frame, and each flower motif was cut roughly from a tracing made of the design, and spaced over the satin. A darning stitch outline was made for each flower through paper and fabric and the paper torn away. Any machine embroidered details could then be completed in the hoop. Using a double sided adhesive tape the template pieces were stuck to the velvet which was to be applied, taking care with the direction of the pile, and each was cut out meticulously.

Because pins can mark velvet the adhesive tape was used again to apply the pieces to the ground. This also prevented slipping and made adjustment easier. The leaves were tacked firmly with a fine needle and 50 thread, and when the hand embroidery on the flowers was completed they were applied in the same way. There is no means of removing crush marks made by a tambour frame on thick velvets so all the pieces had to be satin stitched with the presser foot. After preliminary experiment even this was found to make a permanent mark, and so the presser foot pressure was reduced until no mark remained and tight curves were easier to negotiate. The handmade cord, the beading and the flower centres were all added when the machining was finished. $\times \frac{1}{16}$ actual size.

A floral grouping for fine linear stitchery and delicate appliqué was transferred onto white silk. The photograph shows the ground fabric being used iike a tracing, with both drawing and fabric taped to the window. In this case creamy poster paint and a fine brush were used, but a hard sharp pencil is better on anything other than a smooth fabric.

Direct working is best for nets, perhaps with the addition of outline planning with a tacked line. But if repetitive accuracy is demanded the preliminary shapes can be stitched through both tracing and net and the paper torn away. If detail is attempted by this method the easy flow of the stitchery is stunted and the bits of paper left between the stitches are very difficult to remove.

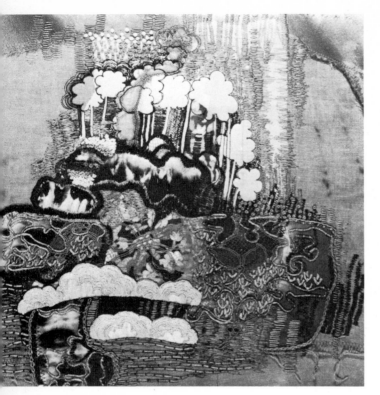

The tambour frame creates several difficulties none of which is insurmountable. When the embroidery is larger than the frame the work cannot be seen as a whole whilst stitchery is being added, so sometimes the work must be lifted away from the machine and spread out for reappraisal. Tacking can fray and disrupt fine appliqué and small pieces as the work is handled, so they must be added gradually, perhaps using small safety pins. If the appliqué is meant to be flat (and there is no logical reason why it should be providing intention is satisfied) it must be firmly secured, and the ground can be cut away behind it afterwards to resolve conflicting fabric tensions. The frame can be moved about the fabric without removing the whole piece from the machine and without constant re-adjustment of the outer ring; this is one instance where a metal frame is impractical because it does not slip together like wood or plastic ones.

Move from one part of the frame to another with care, raising the presser foot bar to release the tension and loosening the cotton before lowering the bar to begin at the new point. Threads can sometimes be finished off by tying, sometimes with a few very close stitches, and zigzag with a few straight stitches. Coarse work can merely be trimmed, cutting the right side first so that the slight tension of cutting the wrong side brings the ends of the top thread through.

It can often be an advantage to work on applied pieces before they are stitched to the main ground fabric, and these can be backed with iron-on *Vilene* either before or after stitching to make their edges easier to deal with. The characteristics of soft fabrics are changed by iron-on *Vilene* and this must be considered. Some backings consist merely of an adhesive ironed on through a paper backing which is then removed. These can be useful for temporarily attaching applied pieces to the ground, but the ironing process involved in softening the adhesive can again flatten and stiffen the fabric. Three step zigzag, a modification on many machines, is a useful means of sewing down. $\times \frac{1}{16}$ actual size.

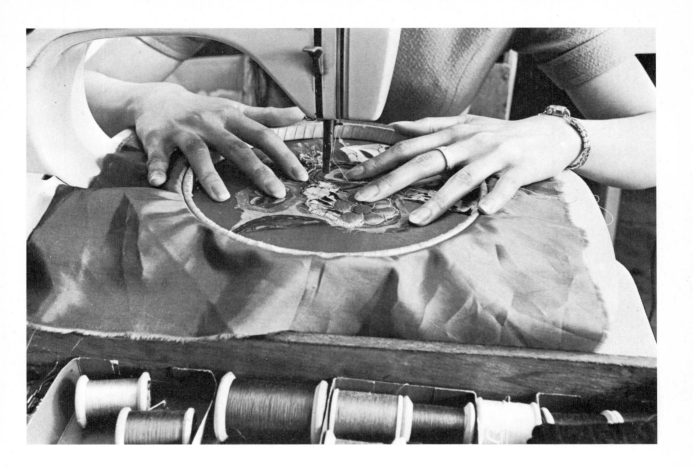

Experience brings the fingers closer to the needle for greater control. If the fabric is bouncing in the tambour frame so that the needle frequently fails to pick up the spool thread then try a more openly woven fabric which will not be lifted by the needle on its upward movement, or use a smaller frame to reduce the surface area of the fabric.

Some embroiderers use stiffening and the darning foot more frequently than the frame, basting the stiffening to the back of the fabric first or using an adhesive lining. Vanishing muslin, a stiffened openly woven fabric, can be singed away with a hot iron when the embroidery is completed. It is not an over simplification to state that the iron is a destructive instrument where embroidery is concerned. Obviously it is necessary for the preparation of fabrics and the use of adhesive backings, but if finished stitchery must be ironed it should be done gently from the wrong side on a very soft padding.

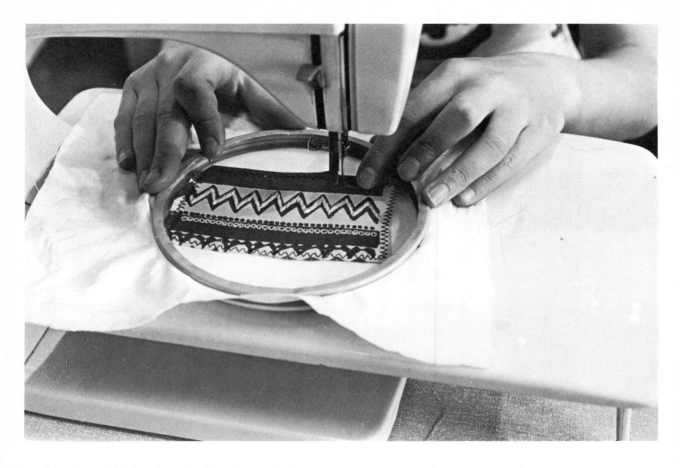

If the piece of fabric to be embroidered is smaller than the frame, machine stitch a fabric of the same weight to it with the raw edges uppermost and cut away the ground from beneath the small piece, so that the whole is as flat as possible to the throat plate.

Some fabrics have a weave which is easily disturbed by tightening in a tambour frame, a tendency avoided by including a piece of fine, strong cotton between it and the inner ring and then cutting away the area of cotton inside the frame. A piece can be prepared and kept specially for this purpose by stretching it alone in the frame, stitching firmly and closely around its perimeter and then cutting away the circle of cotton inside the stitching. This retains a firm shape for future use.

PLATE 3   Crab panel. Padding built up separately from the ground. (See details illustrated on pages 41 and 83). *Private collection*

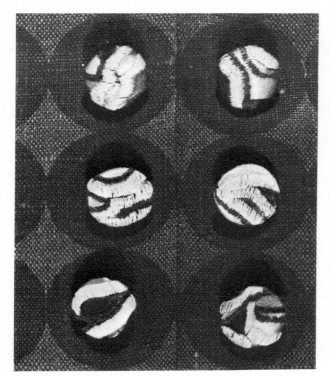

MAKING BUTTONS

Fabric heavy weight rayon furnishing satin with a formalised flower print

Thread 40 *terylene* and 50 embroidery

Tension a slack needle thread and a tighter spool thread, for even zigzag

Needle 90

Choose the button size and draw button rounds on the fabric with white crayon leaving adequate space for mounting between each. Using free stitching and a tambour frame make the widest satin stitch across the rounds, varying to accommodate the patterns of the fabric in each case, and travelling well beyond the perimeter of the circle. Rethread the machine with 50 cotton and reduce the stitch width to half of the previous satin stitch lines. Add this smaller stitch in equal amounts on each circle. Cut out each button cover leaving plenty of material and then mount it in the usual way.

PVC AND LEATHERS

Stitching on leather or PVC is often easier than it appears. Very shiny PVCs can be lightly oiled on the right side (a special oil is manufactured for this purpose) to prevent sticking under the presser foot, or they can be stitched through tissue paper. Use a number 100 needle for heavier leathers or one designed specially for the purpose. A simple appliqué technique seems most appropriate to these materials. Both applied and ground fabrics on the pocket of this apron are leather-look PVC with a strong cotton backing. The shapes are held in place with a small quantity of glue or double sided adhesive tape or other bonding material. The satin stitch completely surrounds each shape, working with very little pressure on the presser foot.

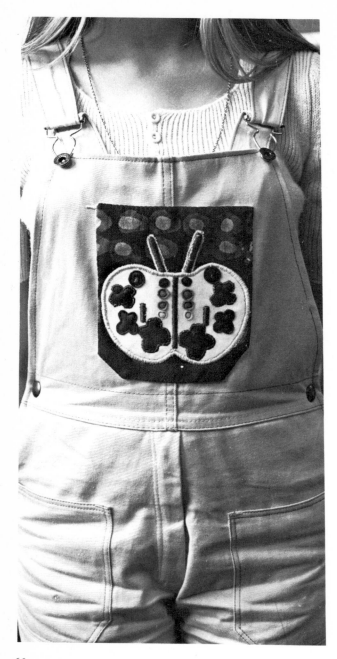

The bib and braces are primary yellow with another pocket patch, this time a white velvet butterfly with red, yellow and lime spots on a deep green, blue and lime wax resist cotton ground. The felts ran very slightly when machine washed, but the wax resist did not. For embroidery on dress or anything which needs laundering washability must be considered for all the fabrics, yarns or beads used. No colour is permanently light fast, hessians, rayons, felts and home dyed colour being especially fugitive subjects.

Fabrics with bias stretch are easily distorted, especially by the presser foot, and need patient experiment to find a suitable technique. Stiffenings of any kind used on clothing will disturb drape and behaviour of fabrics, but backing with vanishing muslin is one solution, and it can be torn or ironed away after stitching.

Sometimes the background fabric can be cut away beneath applied pieces to prevent the fabric becoming too stiff to drape, but total strength must be maintained. Too much stitching in one direction will distort linens and weaken rayons. Stretch towelling can be prevented from bagging by concentrating the decoration on small, compact areas of fabric equidistant from one another, or using a coarse zigzag. Interesting results can be obtained by intentional bagging. The use of a thicker thread will prevent the almost total disappearance of stitchery on some pile fabrics.

A form of gathering not unlike smocking can be achieved by using various colours of 40 cotton in the needle and shirring elastic on the spool.

5 Openwork and quilting

OPENWORK ON FINE FABRICS *(overleaf)*

Fabric   crisp white nylon, multiple embroidered previously with shiny, white synthetic thread
Thread   50, baby blue
Tension   top tension slackened to form the stitch loop on the wrong side of the fabric
Needle   70

An old electric treadle machine is easiest to control slowly and therefore best for this technique. This kind of machine embroidery probably owes more than any other to the traditions of lace and fine stitchery.

Close double circles of stitchery of varying sizes are distributed inside the existing floral pattern. (The circles can be single on closely woven fabrics which are not liable to fray easily.) White printed motifs from a cotton voile are cut with plenty of spare fabric around them and applied flat, so that they destroy the dominance of the multiple spray pattern. The voile is more loosely woven and so needs three lines of stitchery. The whole embroidery is then removed from the frame, the applied pieces being cut away outside the stitchery, and the circles being trimmed close to the inside of the stitchery, with sharp-pointed scissors. The ground is now fragile and must be reframed gently. The openwork fillings are completed first, stitching slowly across the circle and zigzagging over its edge to reach the point for the next diagonal. Where lines intersect a single stitch backwards keeps the junction in place. For the radiating filling with an inner circle a diagonal has been split by single stitches from the outside edge of the larger circle. After the filling for each circle is completed, a thick thread, in this case *coton à broder*, is couched around the edge with a close zigzag. This helps to strengthen the circle and builds a slightly deeper texture to conform with the scale of the rest of the stitchery. The zigzagging is still done with a straight stitch, moving the frame sharply from side to side and turning it periodically so that the movement can continue sideways as the stitching describes the circumference. The eyelets are made with a longer single stitch, having first pierced a centre hole with a stiletto or wider needle. Most machines have to be hand controlled for eyeletting, the slowest speed is still too fast for really accurate control. Each eyelet must be close to a stitched edge where it can be begun and fastened off unobtrusively. The embroidery must be kept neat at the back and carefully trimmed and finished. Each openwork circle is surrounded by a hand stem stitch in dull lilac stranded cotton, and the tiny seed pearls are added last. × 2 actual size.

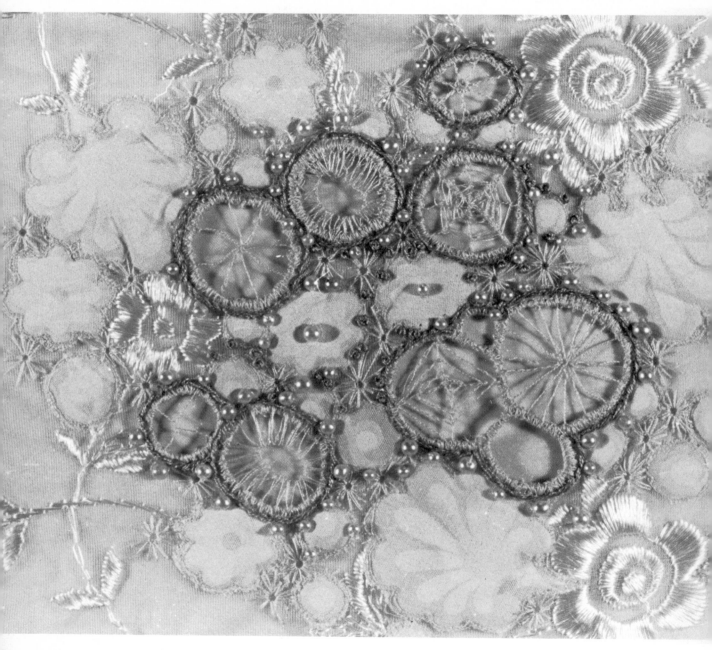

Fabric fine white open muslin with cut pile dots
Thread 50
Tension top tension slackened to form the stitch loops on the wrong side of the fabric.
Needle 70

If free zigzagging and satin stitch are too difficult to achieve linear openwork can be done without them. The stitches in the air must run over the edges of the circles into the fabric, where they can become part of added surface decoration.

Similarly, if eyelets prove insurmountable, machine made ones can be cut from other fabrics and stitched to the ground. This example contrasts the central free stitched ones with the applied pink eyelets to either side, and the larger motifs cut from an old piece of machine made broderie anglaise on white lawn. It is not the purpose of this book to discuss machine accessories, but it should be mentioned at this point that eyelets can be made automatically on a zigzag machine with an attachment.

The technique of applying tiny pieces of delicate fabrics is not difficult once full control of the machine is achieved. It can be at its most beautiful on nets, which are simple to embroider. Openwork and net embroidery are both eminently suitable for precious garments such as Christening robes and bonnets and veiling. On a coarser scale they can be used for soft blouses, evening wear and translucent curtaining and screens. × 2 actual size.

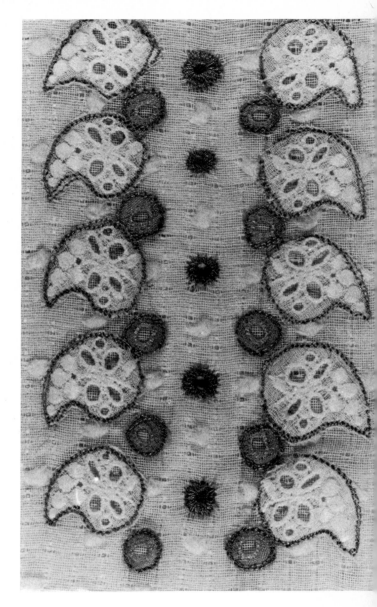

NETS AND ORGANDIE

Many openwork fabrics can be used to make teasing effects of scale by using them in a context where they represent a much larger or smaller texture. This simple landscape drawing, achieved by printing with the nets themselves, indicates a heavily braided lace used to make a boulder strewn slope. The only actual stitchery would be satin stitch and zigzag for the tree trunks. Black net torn up into small pieces makes the leafless tree mass. Tearing distorts the net sufficiently to avoid the moiré effect, an optical phenomenon caused by overlaying

nets or organdies. The effect can sometimes be avoided by changing the direction of the grain on each successive overlay. It can, of course, be used to advantage.

Organdie is delicate and easily torn around the frame. This can be prevented by framing another soft fabric simultaneously, as described on page 64.

Good *terylene* or nylon net, as distinct from rayon, can be long lasting for wearable embroidery which is not subject to frequent washing.

70

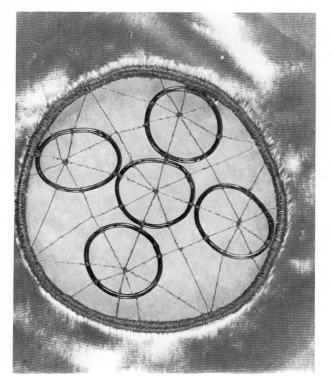

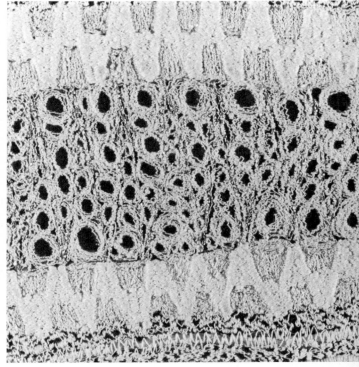

Open textured stitchery is possible on all fabrics, however incongruous the result may be. The scale of the stitching can be used to conform with, complement, or deny, the weave and quality of the ground. Here the stitches suspend brass rings across a hole cut in shiny oyster velvet, a spidery invasion of a sumptuous wardrobe.

Freely used zigzagging of many widths and stitch lengths produces a richness of texture to equal that of precious laces. This is worked on a strong, finely woven, translucent *terylene* of a smokey grey, the eyelets being punched or cut. Embroideries of this kind are extremely strong, and their uniformity of stitch density allows the tambour frame to be moved about the fabric easily. *Example by Judi Lewis.*

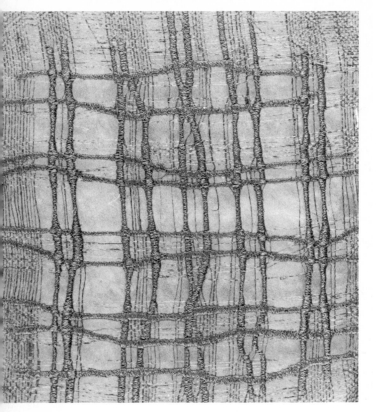
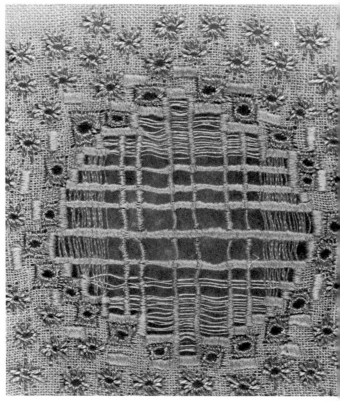

Strong openly woven fabrics like linen scrim present endless possibilities for the enhancement of their own texture or the addition of others. Yarns can be removed in either direction or both, leaving others to be closely gathered or diverted to join new groups. Fine stitchery can be used without embellishment to achieve this, as in the first illustration. The second photograph shows a similar technique used on evenweave linen to imitate traditional drawn thread work, with the addition of hand embroidered eyelets. The ends of applied yarns can be taken through the fabric with a large needle before machining is begun. The stitchery can be built up to dense encrustations, cut away and remounted onto other fabrics, suspended in a spatial context, folded, distorted or padded. With colour interest diminished as far as possible textures become more significant.

Both these pieces are relatively flat and unassuming and so suitable for table linen.

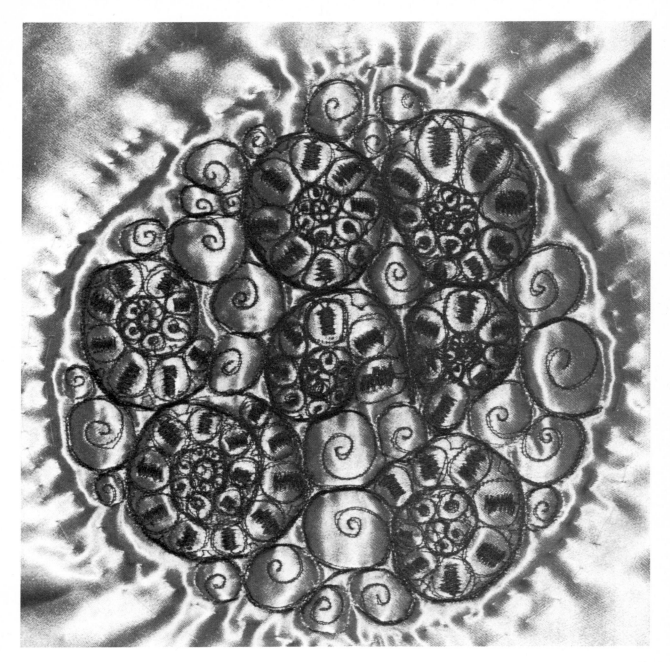

Fabric terylene voile, *dacron* wadding and sage green satin
Thread soft green 50 and colourless monofilament
Tension a tight darning
Needle 90

Machine quilting presents two problems. The design for hand quilting is normally traced onto the backing before the latter is tacked to the other layers, or scratched around a template onto the surface fabric. Machining must be done from the right side for accuracy, and so the design must be scratched, tissue tacked or point marked on that side. Most embroiderers work machine quilting freely with very few guiding marks. The second problem is the confining nature of the tambour frame, which also stretches the fabrics thus preventing characteristic quilting.

This example, worked with only the large circles indicated with scratches, has the major part of its detail stitched before the quilting. With the backing fabric framed only, a circle of *dacron* is cut to fit inside the frame and the previously decorated satin is held loosely over the two. Quilting begins centrally and works outwards, taking care not to pull or pucker the satin. The motif cannot be extended because it is too bulky to accommodate between the rings of the frame, but repeats can be sewn together or incorporated into a larger piece of work.

APPLIED QUILTING

Padded areas can be built up directly onto the ground fabric by applying wadding or domette beneath small pieces of applied fabric. Each enclosed shape needs several rows of close darning stitch. The applied fabric should be roughly trimmed before stitching adjacent shapes, and then closely trimmed with sharp pointed scissors when the embroidery is removed from the frame. An advantage of this technique is that a variety of applied fabrics can be used.

The drawing is from a highly coloured cottage garden/crinoline lady embroidery of the thirties, in padded satin stitch and bullion knots on silk.

QUILTING WITH THE DARNING FOOT

Fabric delicate, powder blue, transparent chiffon, woven with a paler leaf pattern of silk, over two layers of domette backed with white *terylene*.

Thread 50

Tension darning stitch, slightly looser than that used for ordinary sewing.

Needle 80

Continuous areas of free stitching can be done without the frame using the darning foot. Fine fabrics respond best to this technique. All the fabrics are tacked together loosely but at frequent intervals before stitching begins. Quilting shrinks the total measurements of the fabric so a generous allowance is advisable. It sometimes helps to reduce the pressure on the presser foot bar. Control is not precise and the chosen approach should have flow and continuity. The addition of hand stitch-ing or beads gives more textural variety, in this case a heavy chain stitch in soft blue silk. This kind of embroidery is very wearable, soft and warm, and very easy to do.

Monofilament colourless threads can be used to make depressions without a strong line, particularly on felts, which can be stitched through several layers. These threads will not iron, so must be used in the needle and kept on the right side of the fabric so that the embroidery can be ironed on the wrong side. Ironing embroidery is a great mistake and rarely neces-sary, but when it becomes imperative it should be done from the wrong side on a well padded surface.

Quilting experiments with other attachments normally supplied with modern machines, such as the twin needle and the multiple cording foot, are well worth while.

Quilting is often exploited by those needing to employ constructional ingenuity. This idea from a large panel, representing cumulus cloud and taken from a medieval illuminated manuscript, is in graduated blues on a dark ground, highlighted with a thick, white, twisting yarn. Circles of 150 mm (6 in.) diameter are drawn on a pale blue acetate backed with iron-on *Vilene*. A dark wool spirals solidly at the centre, couched with the presser foot, gradually opening into wider and softer zigzagging towards the circumference. The circle is then cut into six radiating sections, each one regularly spaced on the ground and inverted in relation to its nearest neighbour. With edges turned it is stitched and padded firmly. The wool yarn is couched very loosely when all other stitching is completed.

A detail from *The Snow Queen* on page 92 to show one way in which machine embroidered padded shapes can be incorporated into heavy collage and coarse hand stitchery. The embroidery is entirely in smokey blue, greys and silvers. × ½ actual size. *Private collection.*

6 A few more important details

Tie-dye and batik are beautiful end products needing no more embellishment. However, the temptation to use them for embroideries is too strong and often leads to small visual disasters. The simplicity of the stitchery here makes perhaps less of a disaster than many. The cotton fabric has been stitched tightly over folds (a process known as *tritik*), and a newly mixed purple and brown dye bath allowed to absorb at varying rates, making little rocket like explosions across the fabric. A shaded purple-to-pale-lilac 50 thread makes ridges of texture in the same direction, but unlike the tritik it has hard edges and gentle tonal gradation. The underside of a zigzag, with lilac in the needle and purple on the spool, shows at the top of the example. Hand stitchery adds bulky, but still linear texture.

Simple to produce in long lengths, this could be used for borders or ruffles on cotton garments.

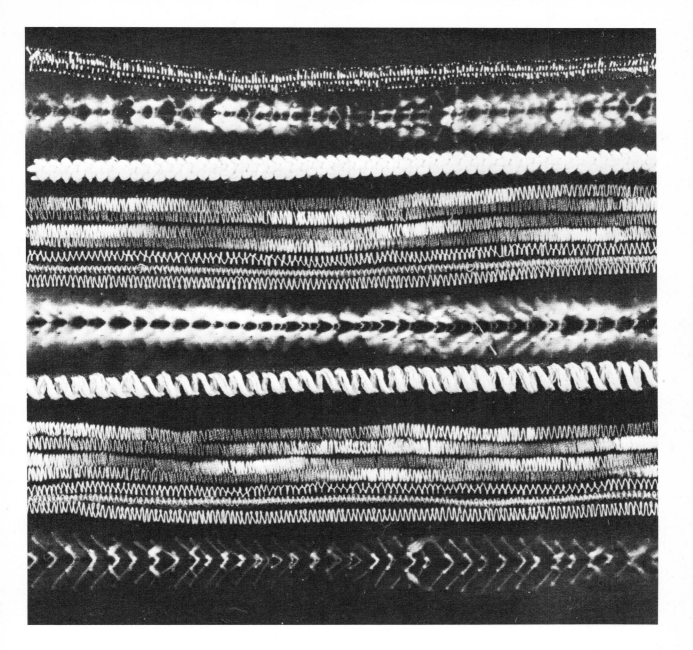

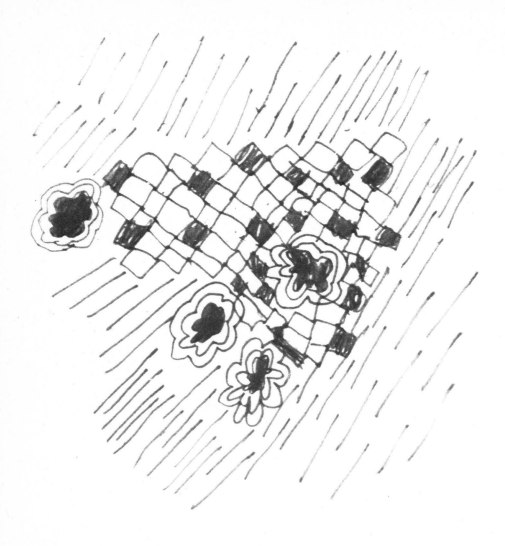

A child's drawing, showing a freedom and freshness of expression which embroidery, being a slow, deliberate process, frequently lacks.

PLATE 4 Flowers cut from stretch *tricel* jersey stitched with free darning to a waistcoat of off-white chenille. The only hand embroidery is wool french knots. This garment has withstood hand washing many times

Stretch fabrics are better avoided at first, they are not easy to handle. For free stitching, they must be flattened in the frame rather than stretched; otherwise when the frame is removed, the stitchery retains its shape while the fabric returns to its original tension. Stitching must be in short lengths with open areas of fabric and small patches of decoration. If the fabric is applied as it is here, then only small pieces are practical. Explore the possibilities of stitching with pressure reduced on the presser foot bar. In this way, a long zigzag can often be incorporated successfully into the natural tension of the fabric. Where a jersey-type fabric is applied to a surface where it will not need stretch (such as a wide skirt hem) it can be backed with fine *Vilene*, tarlatan or muslin before stitching

The Emperor moth, *Saturnia pavonia*, is gregarious throughout its life cycle, and this kind of grouping, drawn from live moths, is characteristic of the species.

Fine appliqué, together with a little hand stitchery, can be used for formalised treatments of natural objects. Choose smooth fine fabrics for the ground, and fine voiles, chiffons or silks for applied pieces. The most comprehensive rag bag falls short of exact colours, so be prepared to use small areas of dye. Tiny quantities of powdered dyes can be mixed with salt in very hot water and painted on. Natural linear structures can be adapted and represented with mainly continuous lines. Give careful thought to representation, so that the essential characteristics of both the object and the medium of the machine are retained. The symmetry of moths and butterflies can be approached by reversing a tracing on either side of a line drawn down the centre of each body.

Finely woven corded fabrics give free machine embroidery a peculiar characteristic. The needle is diverted from a smooth path by the ridges, causing an erratic, tortured line. Judi Lewis has used and emphasised this peculiarity.

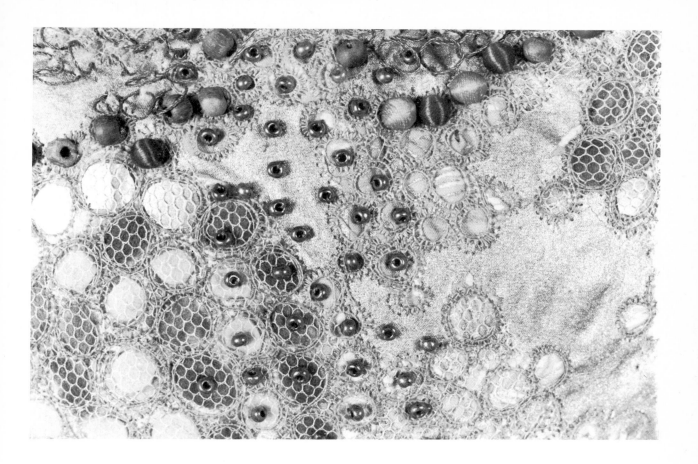

Fabric　closely woven *terylene* with stiff, papery behaviour, richly printed with large, pink and grey-green roses on a gold ground
Thread　30 spool, 50 needle
Tension　feather stitch
Needle　70

This is a detail of the panel shown facing page 64.
Applied circles of orange felt, gold coated paper and flecks of cerise wool are fastened down with repeated circles of feather stitch through net. Some outlying circles have no centres but draw up the fabric making an encrusted surface. The circles are further extended on the fabric alone, accentuating the crustacean texture. Old gold coloured beads, dull wooden beads and tiny satin buttons are applied by hand. A tarnished metal thread is then added by hand, forming each loop around a pencil. × 2 actual size.

Repetitive pattern belongs to all kinds of decoration, and its sources can be found almost anywhere. It should be recognised that exact repeats are not possible in free machine embroidery, in fact it is one of the characteristics of the medium that they are not. For this reason any attractive pattern which does not exactly repeat is worth another look and a glancing analysis. There may be good balance on either side of a central line with many differences in detail which delight the eye. Perfect distribution of weight and texture around a rectangular border may be asymmetrical, with motifs reversed, inverted and adapted. This Scicilian border of soft orange and cream hand chain stitch on a cream linen ground has little discrepancies which grow from the working process and invite closer examination.

Froglet has seen five years of hard wear. On green and blue batik circles of varying shiny fabrics and sequins were surrounded by darning stitch through a layer of net. The net was cut away afterwards and a few deep blue french knots added. Froglet was made up with dried beans inside and given protuberant green glass eyes. His trajectory is very froglike. The stitchery and net have withstood long hours of handling and many washes.

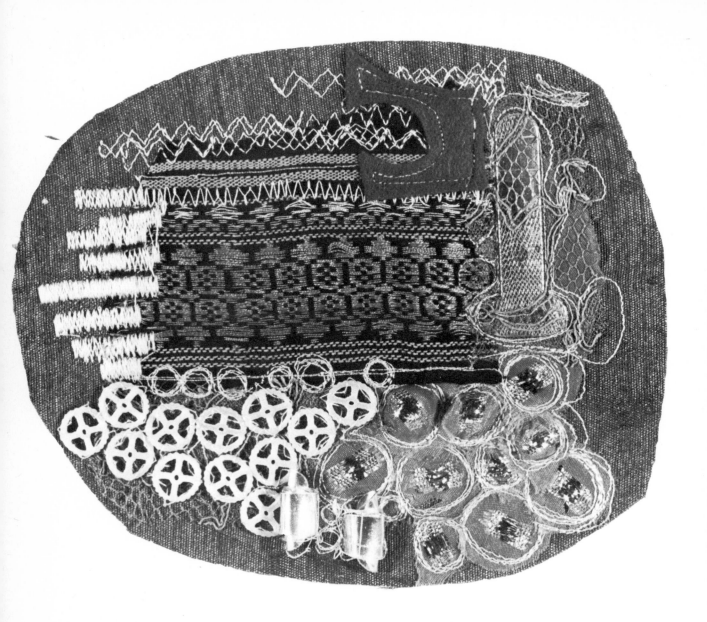

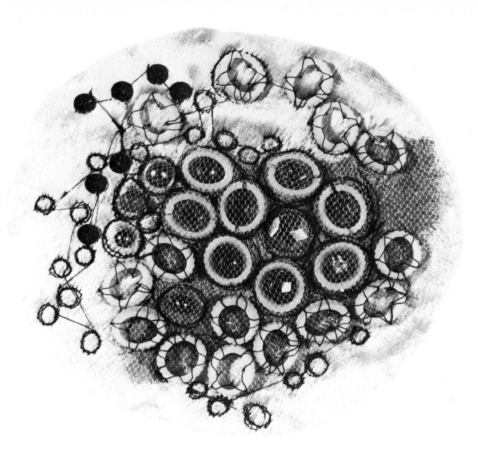

Small objects can be sewn down very quickly by machine. Choose a ground which is easy to handle, preferably with an exciting colour and texture. Choose a small selection of scraps of fabric, pieces of metal, beads, metallic threads and paper, seeds, pastas, pieces of triplex (shattered windscreen), and develop the embroidery from the first idea which occurs.

Experimenting with quite ridiculous materials and inappropriate techniques leads to a much wealthier vocabulary of sound and sophisticated ideas. These particular pieces are cut from the frame, backed with iron-on *Vilene* and trimmed, then glued with a PVA adhesive to the front of a greetings card blank.

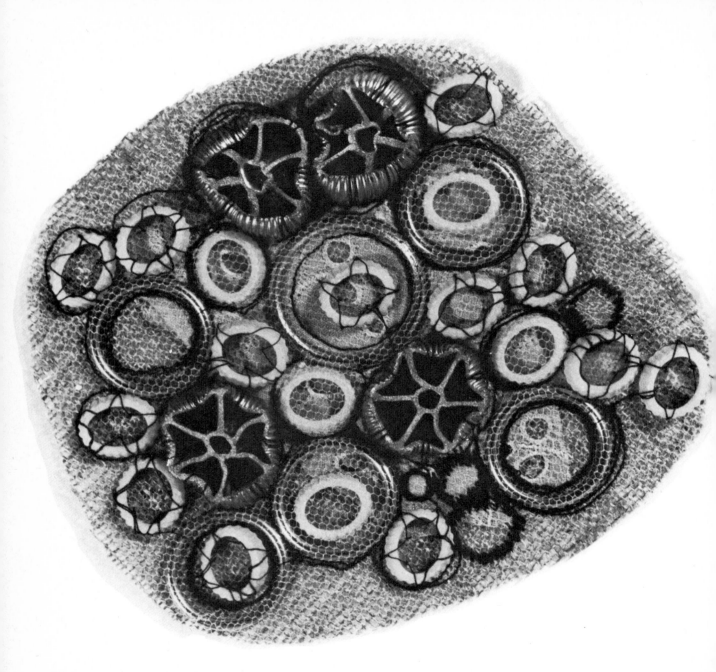

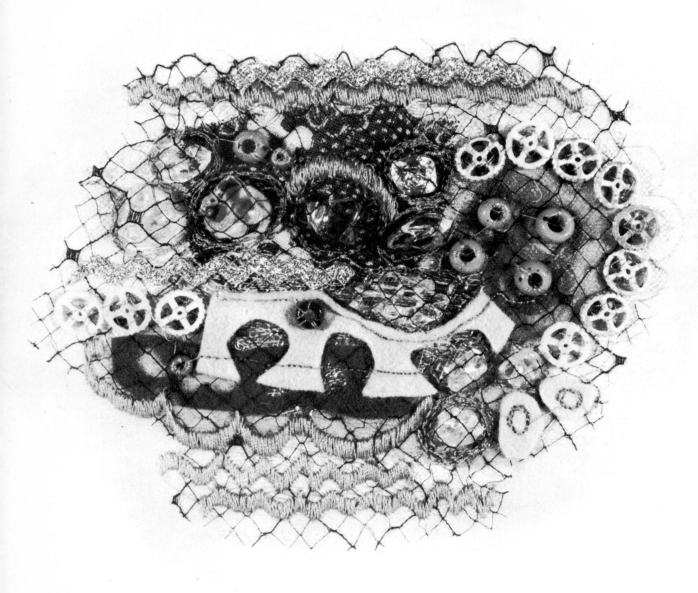

The Snow Queen, a detail of which is shown on page 77. A dense combination of hand and machine stitchery with richly textured collage in silvers, whites and greys. The features are machine embroidered and painted, kept very understated and flat in treatment. The hair is smoke blue enkalon, applied with many tiny stitches. The borzoi dog, a hand-made toy in wood and fur, led to the development of the panel.

Many embroideries need to be displayed behind glass, *Perspex*, *Plexiglass* or clear acetate. Stitchery almost always has considerable depth, so there must be a space between ground and glass, either by making an inner frame or enclosing the whole piece in a box. Dust proofing can be prolonged by the use of appropriate adhesives, foam strips and adequate taping behind the panel. Non-reflecting glass has obvious advantages, but can soften detail. Completely enclosing *Perspex* enhances embroideries, and becomes part of their structure rather than an obtrusive addition. Acetate bubbles are less permanent and more vulnerable, but do allow a wider view.

Suppliers

GREAT BRITAIN

Machines

Machines may be purchased only from authorised stockists.
A list of these appears monthly in the national major sewing
magazines. See also the Yellow Pages of the telephone directory

Information from

Bernina Sewing Machines
50–52 Great Sutton Street
London EC1

Husqvarna Limited
High Lane
Stansted, Essex

Necchi Great Britain Limited
Titchfield House
69–85 Tabernacle Row
London EC2A 4BB

The Singer Company (vic) Limited
255 High Street
Guildford
Surrey

Attachments, needles and spools
From agents supplying machines

**Embroidery threads and accessories including embroidery rings,
hoops and frames, also fabrics**

Mrs Mary Allen
Turnditch, Derbyshire

E J Arnold and Son Limited
(School Suppliers)
Butterley Street
Leeds LS10 1AX

Art Needlework Industries Limited
7 St Michael's Mansions
Ship Street
Oxford OX1 3DG

The Campden Needlecraft Centre
High Street
Chipping Campden
Gloucestershire

Craftsman's Mark Limited
Broadlands, Shortheath
Farnham, Surrey

Dryad (Reeves) Limited
Northgates
Leicester LE1 4QR

B Francis
4 Glenworth Street
London NW1

Fresew
97 The Paddocks
Stevenage
Herts SG2 9UQ

Louis Grossé Limited
36 Manchester Street
London W1

Harrods Limited
London W1

Thomas Hunter Limited
56 Northumberland Street
Newcastle upon Tyne
NE1 7DS

Mace and Nairn
89 Crane Street
Salisbury, Wiltshire

MacCulloch and Wallis Limited
25–26 Dering Street
London W1R 0BH

The Needlewoman Shop
146–148 Regent Street
London W1R 6BA
. also kapok)

Nottingham Handcraft Company
(School Suppliers)
Melton Road
West Bridgford
Nottingham

Christine Riley
53 Barclay Street
Stonehaven
Kincardineshire AB3 2AR

Royal School of Needlework
25 Princes Gate
Kensington SW7 1QE

The Silver Thimble
33 Gay Street
Bath

J Henry Smith Limited
Park Road, Calverton
Woodborough
nr Nottingham

Mrs Joan L Trickett
110 Marsden Road
Burnley, Lancashire

Kapok
Main branches of F W Woolworth and Co Limited

French chalk
Main branches of Boots The Chemists

Vanishing muslin
MacCulloch and Wallis Limited
25–26 Dering Street
London W1R 0BH
Department stores

Leather, gold and silver kid
The Light Leather Group
16 Soho Square
London W1

Suede and leather offcuts
Redpath Campbell and Partners Limited
Department CH13
Cheapside
Stroud, Gloucestershire

USA

Machines
Machines may be purchased only from authorised stockists.
A list of these appears monthly in the major sewing magazines.
See also the Yellow Pages of the telephone directory

Embroidery threads and accessories
Appleton Brothers of London
West Main Road
Little Compton
Rhode Island 02837

American Crewel Studio
Box 553 Westfield
New Jersey 07091

American Thread Corporation
90 Park Avenue
New York

Bucky King Embroideries Unlimited
121 South Drive
Pittsburgh
Pennsylvania 15238

Craft Yarns
PO Box 385
Pawtucket
Rhode Island 02862

F J Fawcett Co
129 South Street
Boston
Massachusetts 0211

Lily Mills
Shelby
North Carolina 28150

The Needle's Point Studio
7013 Duncraig Court
McLean
Virginia 22101

The Thread Shed
307 Freeport Road
Pittsburgh
Pennsylvania 15215

Yarn Bazaar
Yarncrafts Limited
3146 M Street
North West Washington DC

Leather, gold and silver kid
Aerolyn Fabrics Inc
380 Broadway
New York